ST. THÉRÈSE AND SUFFERING

ST. THÉRÈSE AND SUFFERING

SUFFERING

THE SPIRITUALITY OF ST. THÉRÈSE IN ITS ESSENCE

BY

ABBÉ ANDRÉ COMBES

PREFACE BY

MONSIGNOR VERNON JOHNSON

TRANSLATED FROM THE FRENCH EDITION BY

MONSIGNOR PHILIP E. HALLETT

NEW YORK

P. J. KENEDY & SONS

Nihil Obstat:

EDUARDUS GALLEN,
Censor Theol. Deput.

Imprimi Potest:

✠ IOANNES CAROLUS,
Archiep. Dublinen.,
Hiberniæ Primas.

DUBLINI, *die* 14° *Novembris, anno* 1951.

CONTENTS

PREFACE

THE widespread appreciation with which *The Spirituality of St. Thérèse*, by M. l'Abbé André Combes, was recently received, has encouraged the publishers to give to the public the companion volume by the same author, entitled *St. Thérèse and Suffering*. Originally, in France, these two books were published separately, later they were combined in one big volume under the title *An Introduction to the Spirituality of St. Thérèse*: in the English translation the original two-book plan has been adopted as being more practical for English readers.

In the first book the author dealt with St. Thérèse's sanctity in general; in the second volume he addresses himself to one special factor which more than any other went to the perfecting of her sanctity—namely *suffering*.

This study of St. Thérèse and Suffering is not given us in the form of a theoretical treatise, it is, on the contrary, a careful historical examination of certain stages and events in her life, from her first infancy to her death at the early age of twenty-four. At the death of her mother, when Thérèse was only four and a half years old, we are shewn this tiny child face to face with the most poignant sorrow that can befall a little one. She meets it calmly and quietly without a word to anybody.

From this moment onwards, life became for St. Thérèse a question of relating her own weakness to the providential plan of suffering which Almighty God gradually opened up before her. At first she shrank from it, then she came to desire it, finding in it untold treasures; later, it became for her the supreme means of union with God and therefore of perfection; finally she passes beyond this point, and, indifferent either to suffering or joy, she surrenders herself to the merciful Love of God, resting securely in His Holy Will.

This story of the transfiguration of suffering through a simple correspondence with grace, will have its message for everyone who reads it, for we all have to suffer.

St. Thérèse has been raised up for us as a beacon light in the midst of the gathering storm. This book will help us to comprehend that light more clearly and under its guidance to make with safety the harbour of our home in Heaven.

VERNON JOHNSON.

CHAPTER I

" A Desire to Suffer. . ."—St. Thérèse

I.—From January 2nd, 1873, to May 8th, 1884.

IT is suffering, no doubt, that is the gravest danger to, and the hardest test of our poor human love. It is only too true to say that no one attains to self-knowledge until he has suffered. It is still more certain that no one's character is revealed to others until they know the place that suffering has occupied in his life, the way in which he has received this usually unwelcome visitor, and its influence upon his teaching and upon his conduct.

At the point to which we have come in our study of St. Thérèse, however deeply we seem to have penetrated into her soul, if we still remain in the slightest obscurity as to her relation to suffering—I mean to say, as to the manner in which she looked upon it and reacted towards it—we could not flatter ourselves that we had penetrated to the very core of her spirituality.

Such then is the problem we still have to examine. To prove that it is delicate, would be a waste of time. We must remark, however, that it is not new; but though many writers have given their solutions, there is not one that can be called strictly exact. That is the position, and now we must brace ourselves to the effort of discovering the truth.

Everyone agrees, of course, that Thérèse suffered, suffered much and suffered well. We can go further. The formal declarations of the saint herself,[1] those of her companions,[2] those of her biographers,[3] those of the commentators upon

[1] *A.* p. 154: "My soul has experienced many kinds of trials: I have suffered much here below."

[2] *A.* p. 211: "St. Thérèse suffered much here below: towards the end of her life she bade us make this known after her death."

[3] *Cf.* Laveille (*op. cit.* p. 297) and Fernand Landet, *Ste. Thérèse de Lisieux,* 1927, p. 85.

(See p. 133 for Key to References.)   I

her teaching,[1] all converge towards the description of a
definite attitude in the face of suffering, and also towards a
fundamental principle at the base of that attitude. Recently
Père Petitot[2] found an expressive formula for that attitude:
" Smiling in suffering, through love "; and Père Martin[3]
drew up not only the most concise summary of that principle,
but of the laws underlying it: " It is for all these reasons that
suffering is the inseparable companion of love."

Further, no one until the late Canon Paul Travert, the
best interpreter, as it seems to me, of Thérèse's thoughts,
whose loss we all regret, expounded the theology of the
saint on suffering. His pregnant and well-documented pages
on the origin and purpose of suffering are to be found in a
collection of Teresian studies[4] in which an anonymous
writer, also very well-informed, had previously tried to
describe " the reactions set up by sorrow—under whatever
form it came to her—in the soul of St. Thérèse of the Infant
Jesus " with a view to attacking " the exaggerations which
often seem to find a place " in this matter.[5]

Nevertheless, it is strange that no one seems to have thought
of studying, in Thérèse's mind itself, the progressive idea
that she conceived of suffering in proportion as new occasions
of suffering came into her life. Thus all the studies that
have been published, whatever their respective merits,
seem abstract and somewhat unreal. Hence, also, in
proportion as they have thought of Thérèse, not as the author
of a static doctrine given her once for all, but as a living
being subject to organic development and evolution, they
have not escaped error. That is why the question should
be thoroughly investigated yet again. For want of sufficient
attention and fidelity to the texts, even the best interpreters
have often gone astray. I am not speaking merely of those
biographers or theologians for whom Thérèse does not

---

[1] Petitot, op. cit. p. 229.

[2] Op. cit. p. 262.

[3] La Petite Voie d'enfance spirituelle (p. 79).

[4] Travert: La souffrance, son origine et son rôle d'aprés Ste. Thérèse de l'Enfant Jésus,
in Études et Documents Thérèsiens, 1935, pp. 65-75.

[5] C. . . De l'attitude de Ste. Thérèse . . . en face de la souffrance, ibid: 1932,
pp. 50-56, 75-80.

count except in her last years when, as they think, she had become thoroughly herself. Such a limited interest is not the best means to obtain the deepest knowledge of her doctrine. It is a philosophic principle, at least as old as Aristotle, that for full comprehension it is not enough to know only the final form of a thing, but also its genesis and development.

Still less am I thinking of those writers who have no interest whatsoever in chronological order, but pick out texts here and there in Thérèse's writings, just as it suits their immediate purpose.

But I note with regret that even those writers who are most alive to the development of Thérèse's thoughts, and most anxious to follow it through all its phases, have not reached the point to which their method, rightly applied, should have brought them.

There are two chief reasons for this. The first is that they have over-simplified this development and left out intermediate stages which, when discovered, are at once seen to be essential.

The second is that, whereas their method required them to stress the importance of Thérèse's second period—from the age of four and a half to fourteen—and to show its special meaning, they judged this truly important period a little too hastily. They mutilated a very complex whole, for part of it remained unknown to them. Such a misunderstanding is a grave hindrance to a full understanding of Thérèse's attitude to suffering.

To avoid this fault, we must examine, a little more methodically than has been done hitherto, this all-important element of Thérèse's life. We must try to clarify its component parts, their combination, and the final solution of the problem.

To get our bearings, let us first consider the two directions in which our surest guides advise us to travel.

If by them we can reach our end, any new search will be superfluous. If they fail to give us what we want, it will be most instructive to study the reasons for that failure.

The way to find a new route which may lead to success where so many others have failed, is not to analyse the poorest and weakest answers that have been given to the problem, but to see where the strongest and best have gone astray.

We are trying to describe Thérèse's attitude to suffering. We are trying to define as exactly as possible the place that suffering filled in her life and to connect her sufferings with her teaching.

Everyone must agree that our best guide will be Thérèse herself, all the more so as it is precisely in reference to the problem of suffering that she divided her life into the three periods she puts before her biographers.

Surely this is decisive, and if we ascertain the fact and bow to her authority, we have at hand a ready-made scheme of her development. The anonymous writer last quoted gives the following clear account of the matter:[1]

> "St. Thérèse, then, writing at a period (in 1895) when she could in memory take a bird's-eye view of her past life, distinguishes 'three clearly defined periods'[2] in her interior life.
>
> "The first, extending from the dawn of reason until the death of her mother;
>
> "The second, 'the most painful,'[3] including all her childhood until her fourteenth year;
>
> "The third, 'the most beautiful of all, the most richly filled with heavenly graces,'[4] commencing on Christmas Night, 1886."

We could not desire anything clearer. With this information from Thérèse herself, it ought to be possible to draw out a perfectly objective scheme. This, indeed, is what the writer of this remarkable article proceeds to do. We must remark on the three characteristics of his development.

First of all, he holds this threefold division to be adequate and exhaustive. It follows that after the decisive event

---

[1] *Ibid.* p. 51.   [2] *A.* p. 33.   [3] *A.* p. 44.   [4] *A.* p. 87.

of Christmas, 1886, there is no more for the historian to
record. His search is ended. Why? Because "from the
time of this outpouring of grace which begins the definitive
phase of her life" Thérèse is considered to have taken up
a well-defined position without further development. Time
and progress need not now be taken into consideration, for
she remains stationary. Her state of soul can be described
accurately by a consideration of the four qualities which
" sum it up and give us the secret of its calmness and power;
humility, faith, hope and love." [1]

Secondly, he treats the whole of the second period of
Thérèse's life, from the age of four and a half to fourteen,
as homogeneous. This position has the gravest consequences.
The long period of nine and a half years which led to the
event that Thérèse calls her " Christmas grace " is considered
as of one tissue and as capable of being summed up under
one simple description. Her " Christmas grace " is to be
interpreted in the light of this view of the preceding years.

After the death of Madame Martin, suffering, hitherto
unknown, attacks Thérèse so violently that it causes
" comparative disorder and disturbance in her moral faculties.
Sentiment, sensitiveness and imagination are developed to
excess and are more powerful than the reason and the will.
The latter faculties are obliged to make great efforts to
regain their ascendancy, and often are beaten in the conflict."
The whole of this lengthy period is presented to us as of a
uniform pattern, " the phase of hard and hidden struggle " [2]
between the higher and the lower faculties, and it is made
clear that the triple alliance of sentiment, sensitiveness and
imagination generally win the victory against the weaker
coalition of reason and will.

That being the case, Christmas 1886 is represented as
finally restoring equilibrium by a " complete metamorphosis." [3]
After that transformation, the victory abides. " From that
happy hour Thérèse was filled so utterly with the single love
of God and of souls that she was now completely detached

---

[1] C. . . op. cit. p. 56. The second part of this study abandons the historical
order in order to collect from Thérèse's writings, traits relevant to these four virtues.

[2] Ibid. p. 53.   [3] Ibid. p. 56.

from herself and no longer belonged to herself in any way."
Henceforth she was " a soul that had reached equilibrium,
harmonious, peaceful, happy and magnanimous."

·   ·   ·   ·

The third characteristic of this analysis is a consequence
of the two we have now considered. It is an unforeseen
consequence, but there is no escape from it. This judgment
upon Thérèse, whilst claiming to be not only objective,
but also as generous as possible, is in reality extremely
severe. It represents the first appearance of suffering in
Thérèse's life as revealing a psychic weakness as serious
as it was lasting—more than a third of so short a life. In
speaking of a favourable resolution of this long crisis, it
assumes that the permanent cause of the long struggle was
a moral disposition that can only be considered as far from
virtuous. This is how the matter is described:

> " Freed now from her pre-occupation with self . . . our
> little saint ceased to consider suffering in so far as it was
> painful to herself. That counted no longer and she thought
> no more of it. Grace was now victorious, and fixed her
> attention and her efforts upon one object alone from which
> henceforward nothing could detach her: ' To love Jesus
> and to save souls that they may love Him.' " [1]

Let us use plain words. If Thérèse, on Christmas night,
1886, was freed from anything, it was from a manner of
meeting suffering, which manner still included self-love and
egotism.

This conclusion is important, more important than it
might seem at first sight, because it claims to be so faithful
to the texts and so natural that I do not know any writer
who, with whatever modifications, is not prepared to
subscribe to it. As one example we may take the study of
Canon Moreau on the moral temperament of St. Thérèse.

---

[1] *Ibid.*

As a study it is well-informed, searching, discriminating, prudent and well-balanced.

There is, however, one difference that we must note. It is important. This master psychologist is unable to accept the idea of a long period of bitter struggle without any joy. He writes as follows, with much understanding:

> " It would be a mistake to think of Thérèse at this time as a child always in tears. She retains always her liveliness of sentiment, and to a certain extent her impressionable temperament is its own remedy. She is more sensitive than ever to the beauties of nature, and to the charms of family life. Her recollections of her life at Les Buissonnets give the impression of the deep and sometimes unrestrained gaiety that is proper to childhood." [1]

Yet he hastens to add: " But always tears were near at hand," for he agrees fully with the anonymous writer that:

> " In this impressionable child, the death of Madame Martin caused a serious upheaval and, as it were, a rupture of equilibrium and constant tendency to grief." [2]

To this " rupture of equilibrium " he attaches an " excessive sensitiveness " or rather " irresistible emotionalism " [3] which weighed heavily upon " the days of greatest gaiety, pleasure, and heartfelt happiness." It cast its dark shadow upon everything: fishing excursions, feasts and even Thérèse's

---

[1] Moreau. *Ste. Thérèse de l'Enfant Jésus. Son tempérament moral.* Paris, 1938. p. 108. Père Piat (*op. cit.* 2. 286, note), owes much to this " powerful psychological study " in his treatment of this question. He speaks of Thérèse's life at Les Buissonnets in terms which accentuate her deliverance. After saying (p. 260): " Her sensitiveness, made keener by her grief, was aroused by the tiniest things," he makes no further comment until he comes to describe the grace of Christmas (p. 280): " She had to get rid of her sensitiveness, her exaggerated keenness of impression, and vehemence of accent which for the most trivial reasons bathed her in floods of tears. Jesus worked the miracle ' on the unforgettable day of Christmas, 1886.' This is what Thérèse in her *Autobiography* calls ' her conversion.' In its psychology it effected a veritable revolution. Thereupon, her interior equilibrium was fully established." Père Piat a little further on (p. 282) comes back to the question and discusses the epithet of " cry-baby."

[2] Moreau, *op. cit.* p. 107.

[3] *op. cit.* p. 70, where these two phrases are used in succession.

first Communion itself.[1]   All the trouble came from her
first sorrow.   It was never quite cured, because:

> " When the wounds of her heart began to heal, they were
> re-opened by new shocks of sorrow.   The greatest was
> the entry of her ' little mother ' into the Carmel." [2]

Her will, nevertheless, continued to struggle, and it is
not the least merit of this careful analysis that it shows
how " this weakness of her emotions was combined with
real strength of will." [3]   Indeed, the will carried on the
struggle so effectively that the " conversion " of Christmas
night was, properly speaking, its victory.

Whether he considers, then, this sudden change as the
defeat of sensitiveness or the victory of the will, this writer's
conclusion is as follows:

> " But all at once this sensitiveness finds itself opposed by
> an opponent which slowly and silently gathers strength
> and then, suddenly raised by grace to new power, calms
> and restrains all its emotions.   This opponent is the
> saint's will.[4]

> " For Thérèse's will had never abdicated before this
> painful sensitiveness.   On the contrary it had continually
> struggled against it, it had gathered together the moral energy
> necessary to a life of constant sacrifice and unweakened
> perseverance, until the day when it had completely conquered
> this sensitiveness, and firmly established in her heart ' the
> need to forget herself always,' and therewith peace and
> happiness.   For the change that took place on that memorable
> Christmas night was no doubt ' a little miracle,' that is
> to say, a precious grace, but it was also, under the influence
> of that grace, the work of her will.   Ten years of struggle
> had been spent in preparing for this victory.   That is why
> it was instantaneous when at last it came." [5]

Here, it is well to note, there is no question of any moral

---

[1] *op. cit.* p. 109.   [2] *Ibid.*   [3] *Ibid.* p. 134.
[4] *Ibid.* p. 110.   [5] *Ibid.* p. 135.

defect, only of a conflict between sensitiveness and will. Thus there is a very great difference between this analysis and the one we considered earlier. Yet they have three characteristics in common which we must now emphasise.

First, the state of Thérèse's soul which was cured on that Christmas night is described as a conflict between the faculties of sentiment and will, as they normally interact on the natural level. It was merely because she had to get the better of an exaggerated sensitiveness that her will had to struggle and sometimes to own to defeat.

Secondly, this struggle lasts throughout the whole of what Thérèse calls the second period of her life—ten years.

Thirdly, this long period is strictly homogeneous in its nature. On this cardinal point, the words of Père Moreau leave no room for doubt:

> " The crisis of sadness, which began when she was four, lasted ten years." [1]

There is no ambiguity. Whichever writer we consult, we are invited unhesitatingly to think that during ten long years, St. Thérèse could not overcome the sadness that a cruel grief had brought to her sensitive heart—a sadness that was kept alive by other repeated griefs.

As the reason of her inability to overcome it, some writers suggest that we should diagnose some kind of moral defect.

---

[1] *Ibid.* p. 110. The late lamented Canon Lahitton made a careful analysis of the " Deep Thoughts of St. Thérèse " in *Études et documents Thérèsiens* (Vols. III-VIII, 1935-1939). It is curious to note that he makes no direct decision upon the nature of Thérèse's upheaval. In volume III, p. 115, all that he says is: " After the death of her mother the young child underwent a psychological change, which it is not rare to find in children of that age." He goes on to describe the " Second Period " (up to his article of April 1939) as if the events occurred, not in accordance with any fixed law, yet all as conditioned by her trouble. It is only when he arrives at the great grace of Christmas that he is obliged to define in what the trouble consisted. We find then that he too regards the second period as of one nature throughout, morbid sensitiveness being continuously predominant. (Vol. VIII, Ap. 1939, p. 50): " During six years she suffered from a morbid sensitiveness which clogged her progress. No effort seemed able to cure her. With this unfortunate disposition, more physical than moral, it was impossible to hope that she might enter the Carmel. The religious life, especially during the novitiate, is a perpetual warfare with self. It demands strong characters and not weak whiners." He represents the grace of Christmas (p. 52) as the resumption by the will of control over the emotions.

2

All, at any rate, agree that this sensitive child suffered from
an inward disorder which must be attributed to the excessive
liveliness of her impressions, to the powerlessness of her
will to establish control without an enormous discharge of
energy, in a word, to a characteristic psychic disorder.

That being agreed, all these writers go on to state that the
progress Thérèse herself declared to be necessary if she was
to advance to sanctity, consisted precisely in the re-
establishment of order in her soul. Thus they unanimously
define the grace of Christmas as the restoration, vainly
attempted during ten years, of the normal psychical condition,
viz., the rule of the emotions by the will. This return to
due order, adds the most acute of these interpreters of her
inner life, was obtained by " a supreme effort " of this will
itself, raised with the aid of grace to the highest point of
strength by ten years' preparatory effort.

If we are to believe these historians, the " conversion "
of Thérèse was but the admirable, but difficult, triumph of
her will-power. Thus she was able to cure the internal
disorders caused by her continued powerlessness in the face
of overwhelming sorrows.

This is the account given by acute and capable writers.
But is it true?

The texts certainly suggest that this question is of capital
importance, but they by no means require that we should
answer it in the affirmative.

The importance of the question appears from Thérèse's
own witness to the place of suffering in her spiritual life.

> " My soul has been purified in the crucible of interior
> and exterior trials. Now, like the flower after the storm,
> I can raise my head." [1]

When she wrote these lines in 1895, Thérèse had come to
a time in the history of her soul when she could look back
and see clearly the course of her earlier development. She

---

[1] *A.* p. 31.

compares herself to a flower lifting its head after a storm, or to gold purified by the fire. All her past trials had helped her progress and now she felt that her spiritual life had reached maturity. Some writers, however, have no interest in her teaching except at its full development;[1] they seize upon the ripe fruit, so to speak, in order to pluck it and to taste it. But does one taste doctrine as one tastes fruit? One must know it through and through.

To have full understanding, then, of Thérèse's life and thought in their maturity, we must not neglect the interior and exterior trials that went to their preparation, not separate arbitrarily phases that in truth were continuous, nor fall into error concerning the exact nature and order of succession of these trials. They were the means by which a great saint was brought to maturity. The slightest mistake as to the nature of the mould may lead to the grossest errors as to the soul that has been moulded. What was there, then, in this soul that had to be developed, and how did " the crucible " and " the storm " favour this development?

If we consider two all-important texts, we shall conclude that it is most doubtful whether to this question the correct answer has been given.

The first text shows us that if Thérèse divided her life into three distinct periods, historians are not entitled to assume a break of continuity between them. On the contrary, she realised clearly that they were continuous and by this very characteristic she explained the long years of deep and early suffering:

" As I became so early in life the spouse of Jesus, it was necessary for me to suffer from my very infancy." [2]

---

[1] This attitude of mind is well illustrated by the anonymous writer we have already quoted (C. . . *op. cit.* p. 56): " From the date of her ' conversion ' begins the ' definitive phase ' of her life. It is now that we must study her attitude in face of suffering if we would have a true idea of it." In truth, Thérèse's attitude at the age of four, at the age of eight, twelve or fourteen, is no less characteristic than her attitude at the age of twenty. Progress is the law of life. It is all very well to say that we want the full development, the completed picture. There would be no full development if there were not also beginning and growth. The road to perfection is as important as its termination. The end is conditioned by the means. The historian must never separate the two.

[2] *A.* p. 41. Thérèse repeats the same idea with the rich imagery which is characteristic of her book and, incidentally, has occasioned so many errors of

You see the difference? The psychologists are more concerned with the building up of the character than of God's plan for it, and therefore are blind to almost everything except the disordered equilibrium which has to be overcome and cured. The saint, however, was conscious of the divine law which from the beginning was ruling her whole life. They condemn a weakness which distresses them and needs to be cured; she reveals a trial with a purpose, a preparation not only suitable but even necessary, the educative action of God upon a soul called, as she was, so early in life to be the spouse of Christ.

To state the difference in their point of view is not the same as proving that the psychologists are wrong. We have to decide the problem whether there was a psychic upheaval in Thérèse or only imperfections to be overcome.

If we are to proceed in a purely objective way, we must keep always before our eyes that this little child who was so often moved to tears, was the spouse whom Jesus had chosen and was preparing for Himself by these very sufferings. As soon as we agree upon this fundamental principle, we see the need for caution. Must not suffering permitted by God for such a purpose be somewhat different from ordinary suffering?

The least that we can say is that we must be most prudent. The problem is no simple one. We cannot solve it without care. Many writers have considered only the external side of what is really a subtle interplay of events, thoughts and emotions. We have not only to analyse, upon the natural level, the interaction of the faculties of Thérèse's soul; but we must assume and then discover, as our primary task, the action of God Who makes all suffering subservient to His gracious purposes.

.   .   .   .   .

If, in opposition to the views of her historians, Thérèse

interpretation: " As the early spring flowers begin to come up under the snow and open at the first rays of the sun, so the little flower whose story I am writing had to pass through the winter of trial." The comparison is exact and the law is inflexible. The very earliness of the flower's development demands the premature coming and intensification of suffering.

shows that, in this particular matter of suffering, there was continuity rather than division, during the three periods of her life, yet she excludes still more clearly the notion that the long period between her fourth and fourteenth years was entirely homogeneous in character. Our second text must now be quoted.

On July 31st, 1897, on her bed in the infirmary from which she was not again to rise, the dying saint said to Mère Agnès words which seem designed especially for us:

> " Since my first Communion, when I begged Jesus to change for me all earthly consolations into bitterness, I have always had a desire to suffer." [1]

How is it that such a statement has been overlooked? The context, as we shall see, is still more important than the words, but they are quite clear enough in themselves to prove the historians wrong. For here Thérèse under our very eyes, as it were, spontaneously introduces a fundamental division, a principle of utter diversity, in the course of the long, and supposedly dark and homogeneous, period of ten years. It is worth while looking closer.

Thérèse, we are told, for ten years was subject to some kind of psychic depression during which her morbid sensitiveness was constantly getting the better of her will. Yet we see that here, at the time of her first Communion, that is to say, two years and eight months before her " conversion " at Christmas, 1886, when she is supposed to have gained her long-awaited victory, she makes her resolution in perfect freedom and addresses to her dearly-loved Lord a petition that ought to have caused consternation amongst our psychologists, for it is in no way a preparation for her final victory, at least as they have imagined it.

We cannot insist too much upon this surprising fact. Far from being overwhelmed with the grief they describe to us, this little first communicant finds that there is much too much human consolation in her life. It is on this point that she feels the need of improvement, or of a remedy.

[1] N. V. p. 96.

Why? In order that she may be freed from whatever seems to her sad, depressing, sombre, bitter?

Far from it. Her petition is that Almighty God may exercise His power to turn into bitterness for her all the consolations that it may be possible for earth still to offer her.

In May 1884, if Thérèse suffered from spiritual disorder it was exactly the opposite to that which the historians assign to the period between 1877 and 1886. She considered that she had, not too many trials, but too many consolations. Did she deceive herself? Was she, without suspecting it, the victim of habitual depression? Obviously not, for she quite deliberately sought suffering. Far from reacting with her will against her supposed sorrows, far from wishing to throw off pain and to regain a joy that would allow her to be truly herself, she desires to suffer, as she always desired to suffer.

There is no escaping the conclusion. We have in the words we have quoted a proof that, between 1877 and 1886, there was at least one important change in Thérèse's spiritual life, important enough profoundly to modify the whole of her interior life, and a proof that in considering that long period as strictly homogeneous, historians have gone very far astray.

They are equally wide of the mark when they regard as final the state of mind to which Thérèse attained at her " conversion " of Christmas, 1886. On this point, as on the other, it is strange if they have failed to notice the perfectly clear and explicit information that she gives. When she divides her life into three periods, she is not speaking of her whole life, but only of her life as an infant and a child before she entered Carmel. She says so expressly:

> " In the history of my soul up to my entry into Carmel, I can distinguish three clearly-marked periods." [1]

This three-fold division makes no account of the period which, from the available evidence, we naturally suppose

---

[1] A. p. 33.

to have been the most important, from the point of view of her teaching. Consequently, her life must be divided into at least four periods. There is no reason to think that this fourth period is merely a prolongation of the third and that it can be defined by exactly the same characteristics that she assigned to the earlier one.

Clearly the problem has never yet been correctly stated. Perhaps it is still too early to hope to discover a definitive solution. We must at least try to analyse the data we possess in order to discover what were the mutual reactions in the saint, of suffering and thought.

From earliest infancy Thérèse was no stranger to physical pain. Though she came into the world " strong and healthy," [1] before a fortnight was out her mother was in the gravest anxiety, and thought she was to lose this child as she had lost four others of her children. [2]

After this critical period, the child went on well until the end of February. [3] Then the trouble reappeared in so serious a form that on March 1st all hope of saving the child's life was given up. [4] Unexpectedly, however, the baby had strength enough to survive until a wet-nurse could be found. [5] In the country, in spite of some set-backs, the child's health greatly improved. When she returned to Alençon, April 2nd [6] 1874, she was thriving. [7] She had

[1] *Letter* lxxxi of Madame Martin to her sister-in-law, Jan. 3rd, 1873 (in *Annales de Ste. Thérèse de Lisieux*, 1942, p. 10). Thérèse was born that evening. Her mother " for two months had found that the child was stronger than her previous babies " and expected it would be a boy.

[2] Letter lxxxiii of Madame Martin to her brother the chemist, Jan. 17th, 1873 (*ibid*. p. 13): " I am greatly worried about my little Thérèse. I fear intestinal trouble. There are the same alarming symptoms as with my other children who died. Am I to lose this one also? " The next day she told her sister, the Visitation nun at Le Mans, that death was near.

[3] Letter lxxxiv of Mme. Martin to her brother, March 1st (*ibid*. p. 13): " The poor child is in terrible pain since yesterday. It goes to the heart to see her."

[4] *Ibid*. " She is very ill and I have given up all hope of saving her life."

[5] Letter lxxxvi of Mme. Martin, *ibid*. p. 18.

[6] Piat, *op. cit.* (p. 118).

[7] Letter cxiv of Mme. Martin to her sister-in-law, June 1st, 1874 (*Annales* 1943, p. 8): " I have never had so strong a child, except the first."

much pain when cutting her teeth.[1] Some months later[2]
and then again in October,[3] Madame Martin had further
cause for anxiety.

After that, however, Thérèse went on splendidly until
November, 1876, when she seemed really ill.[4] In January,
1877, her mother complained again of congestion.[5]

But of all these childish complaints or illnesses, Thérèse
seems to have retained no sort of memory. For her earliest
months that is only to be expected. With April, 1873,
however, began the series of letters from Madame Martin
which Mère Agnès put into her hand to aid her recollections.[6]
If Thérèse did not mention these illnesses of her infancy
in her autobiography, it is because she considered that the
sufferings of so early an age formed no part of the history
of her soul. What she preferred to record in these " sun-lit
years " of her infancy[7] was her heart-felt grief and her tears
of contrition whenever she gave way to childish faults and
in any small way surprised or grieved her parents.[8]

[1] Letter cxviii of Mme. Martin to her brother, August 9th, 1874 (*ibid.* p. 19):
" My little Thérèse has been very ill this week. It is true it is only her teeth, but
she has had a very bad time."
[2] Letter cxxix of Mme. Martin to her sister-in-law, May 19th, 1875. (*ibid.*
p. 69): " My little Thérèse is ill; she has fever and a troublesome cough."
[3] Letter cxxxviii of Mme. Martin to Pauline (*ibid.* p. 89), Oct. 10th, 1875:
" Thérèse has been ill for two days, she has fever and stomach trouble." On Oct. 14th
she was still ill (Letter cxxxix in *Annales*, 1944, p. 11). She is said to be well again
on Oct. 24th. (Letter cxl to Pauline, *ibid.* p. 11).
[4] Letter clxx of Mme. Martin to her sister-in-law, Nov. 12th, 1876: " I am worried
about little Thérèse; she seems to suffer from congestion. Whenever she walks
quickly, you can hear a kind of wheeziness in her chest. . . If I should lose this
child, I should be inconsolable."
[5] Letter clxxix of the same, Jan. 8th, 1877: " My little Thérèse is ill, and I am
anxious. She is always having colds and then she gets congested. This usually
lasts two days."
[6] *A.* p. 34: " You were so good, dear Mother, as to put into my hands the letters
mother wrote to you at this time when you were at school at the Convent of the
Visitation at Le Mans." From the edition of Mme. Martin's letters in the *Annales*
it follows that this collection began only from April, 1873. " Earlier letters to her
children have unfortunately not been preserved " (*Annales* 1942, p. 37, note).
It is a serious loss, for Marie and Pauline, the two older children, went to school
at Le Mans in Oct., 1868.
[7] *A.* p. 41.
[8] *A.* p. 35-36: " As soon as she has committed the slightest fault, everyone has
to know about it." " Contrary to my usual custom, I would not move, and cried
out obstinately: ' Come to me, Papa . . .' my cries of contrition at once sounded
through the house." " I don't want anyone to see me . . . her little face was covered
with tears."

If we do not give too much importance to her petty griefs at the absence of her sisters,[1] and to her playing at being ill,[2] we would seem justified in concluding that the only sorrow Thérèse felt in her earliest childhood was the grief of contrition. But that was a sorrow for which she had instinctively found an unfailing remedy: an immediate avowal of her faults, complete repentance and the fullest reparation.[3]

It was an excellent beginning. If God had had no other designs for this child than an ordinary good Catholic life, He need not have done more than allow dispositions so favourable to the normal action of His grace to grow in peace and joy. But His divine providence had far grander plans for her, and these demanded, as Thérèse herself has told us, far greater conflicts.

Thérèse's health was now re-established, her intelligence was developing with abnormal rapidity, " she found flowers all along her way." [4] But now a violent shock came to shake to their foundations the peace and the happiness of her daily life. On August 28th, 1877, her mother died. The next day she kissed her mother's forehead for the last time and bade farewell to the joy, the vivacity and the expansiveness which hitherto had characterised her.[5]

The beginning of her sorrow was the beginning of her weakness. What this weakness was, does not yet seem to have been clearly ascertained by her biographers. If we can improve upon their results, it can only be by taking into account all the texts and treating them with the greatest

[1] Letter clvi to Pauline (May 14th, 1876): " Thursday evening, we walked in the direction of the station. Thérèse insisted on going into the waiting-room to fetch Pauline! She ran ahead, delighted with herself, but when she found that she had to come back and was not able to get on to the train to come to fetch you at Le Mans, she cried all the way back."

[2] Letter clxxii to the same (Dec. 3rd, 1876): " Thérèse saw how happy Céline was when she was ill in bed and very much wanted to be ill with her. Then she really was ill with a high temperature. . . When she was in pain she was asked: ' Are you pleased now to be ill like Céline? ' But no! Now things were different. She answered amidst her tears: ' I wanted to be a little ill—little like the head of a pin—but not like this! ' "

[3] A. p. 35-36.

[4] A. p. 41.   [5] A. p. 43.

attention and respect.   When we know better all the facts, in their detail and variety, we may be able to offer an interpretation more in conformity with the aspirations of Thérèse's soul and with the graces that preceded and followed them.

One thing we must admit at the outset.   Thérèse herself is to a large measure responsible for the unfavourable judgments which her best-informed biographers have passed upon the state of her soul between August 28th, 1877 and December 25th, 1886.   She it is who, in the writings which are immediately accessible to us and easy of interpretation, has exhibited this period as continuous and homogeneous in character.   She it is who, in simple, unambiguous words, has described the permanent nature of the change that came over her.   Clearly and unhesitatingly she has written of the upheaval brought about in her by her mother's death, then of her inability to overcome her extreme sensitiveness, and finally of her sudden and complete cure.

We have only to read her words to understand how competent historians have come to the conclusion that they had but to repeat her own declarations, without thinking of any other interpretation than their obvious one:

> " As soon as my mother died, my character completely changed.   I had been so vivacious, so expansive, but now I became quiet and timid, excessively sensitive.   A single look was often enough to make me burst into tears.   I wanted to pass unnoticed; I could not endure to meet strangers and I could be gay only in the family circle.[1]
>
> " Moreover . . . I felt like an exile, I used to weep and to think how I had now lost my mother.[2]
>
> " I was now so timid and sensitive, that I did not try to defend myself, but merely shed tears in silence.[3]
>
> " I could only get two or three minutes at the end of the family visits to the Carmel. . .   I used to spend them in weeping and then I went away with a broken heart.[4]
>
> " My extreme sensitiveness made me a most tiresome

---

[1] A. p. 44.   [2] A. p. 45.
[3] A. p. 56.   (She refers to her first year at the Abbey).   [4] A. p. 61.

child. All remonstrances were in vain; I could not correct
myself of this ugly defect.[1]
"Little Thérèse had at last regained for ever the strength
of soul which she had lost when she was four and a half." [2]

With these texts before us, how can we fail to conclude
that, during ten years of imperfection, the future saint
lacked strength of will, that she was unable to master her
sensitiveness, that she made herself unbearable by continual
tears, in season and out of season? Surely we are right
in speaking of a psychological disturbance and in dating
the effective call of this weak girl to sanctity from
Christmas, 1886.

We might well be carried away by these logical inferences,
did we not know that there are other writings to be added
to Thérèse's dossier for this period, and that they complete
in a remarkable manner, by new information, the texts
which we have just quoted and which most biographers have
considered to be sufficient.

Yet, even taking these texts alone, we might have found
reasons for caution. Though we know the truthfulness of
their author, we must take account also of her humility.
We must observe, also, that when in two lines she sums up
ten years of her life, she is necessarily giving a very inadequate
simplification of what was necessarily changing and complex.

It is, of course, true that Thérèse represents herself
during this long period of her life as disturbed on account
of the shock of grief at its commencement, and as henceforth
hindered in the practice of virtue. But we must try to
understand more exactly in what consisted this disturbance
and this weakness which for so long she could not overcome.

Now we need not go outside the pages of her autobiography
to see how she suggests prudence to those biographers whom
at first she seems to supply with evidence so clear and
unmistakable. She seems to advise them, if they will but
listen to her, to take every possible precaution before
passing judgment upon the whole of those ten years and the
crisis that comes at their end.

---

[1] *A*. p. 86.   [2] *A*. p. 87.

When she had not yet entered upon these ten years, at the very moment when she was stricken with grief, this was her state of mind, as she afterwards described it:

> "I cannot remember that I shed many tears. I spoke to no one of the deep emotions that filled my heart: I looked on and listened in silence." [1]

By the death-bed of her mother, a new Thérèse was taking form. But how? Was it by a disturbance in the harmony that hitherto had been established between her faculties? Not at all. It was rather by an increase of thoughtfulness and seriousness.

When the sudden blow of grief fell upon her, she shed few tears, she poured out her sorrows to no one. Her dear mother could no longer hear her. To whom should she speak? But though she lost her power of speech, she was not prevented from thinking. Her heart was filled with new emotions. Pent up in her breast, these sentiments were profound, and would ever remain so. [2] Can we know what they were?

As Thérèse did not speak about them at the time, she saw no need to disclose them eighteen years later. One thing, however, is obvious. The deeply affectionate child was brought face to face with a heart-breaking spectacle, and yet the quiet, sober, unadorned words of her description show nothing but complete self-possession.

The little child who loved her mother so much, now sees her dead and understands that she has lost her. At once, her heart is filled with deep emotion, but her eyes shed few tears, her lips allow no word, no complaint, to escape. She sees and hears all that she wills. In circumstances new and unforeseen, when she might well have lost all self-control,

---

[1] A. p. 43.

[2] At the deathbed of her mother, Thérèse's depth of character is first revealed. Canon Lahitton (*op. cit.* t. iv, 1935, p. 18), when he comes to relate the fishing expeditions at Lisieux, says: "Here, for the first time, Thérèse speaks of her deep thoughts." That is quite true, but several months before these meditations the grief that she could not express to herself, still less communicate to others, had come to bring depth to her soul.

she sees or guesses everything. Her behaviour made a deep impression on her sisters, as Marie, later on, declared upon oath:

> " At the moment of my mother's death, Thérèse was marvellous. We had no time to give to her, and she on her side did not try to attract attention to herself. But I was careful not to ask her of what she was thinking for I did not want to deepen still further the deep emotions of which she speaks." [1]

Her biographers have not been so tactful. They have known no more than Marie the state of her little sister's soul; they have not taken the trouble to make absolutely necessary distinctions, and yet they have delivered their formal and exact judgment in a manner that seems to exclude all appeal.

Without going any further we can assert that their judgment has failed to take into account a fact that is essential and as clearly attested and worthy of belief as any other fact of her life. At the moment of her mother's death, at her first meeting with sorrow, Thérèse drew, from her own inner resources, strength to hold back her tears, to suppress all complaints or indiscreet questions. Her heart, instead of giving itself over to passionate grief, gained in depth and seriousness. Where is the loss of harmony? Where is the weakness?

To be able to form a satisfactory judgment upon this psychological problem, we should have needed to live with Thérèse, and not only to watch all her actions, but to have gained her confidence so completely that none of her intentions or reflections would remain unknown to us.

But, whatever we may think of this, in fact no one had

---

[1] Deposition of Sept. 6th, 1910, at the Ordinary Process (*Summ.* p. 114, para. 228). Five years later, on July 20th, 1915, at the Apostolic Process, the same witness added: " When in the Carmel Thérèse was speaking to me of this time of her earliest infancy, she said: ' It seems to me that I judged things just as I would to-day.' " Sœur Marie ended her evidence by giving this noteworthy reason: " I considered her very advanced for her age " (*Summ.* p. 79, para. 141).

that opportunity. From this time, when sorrow deepened her life, Thérèse tells us that she maintained a close reserve upon her most intimate thoughts and feelings. We can only admire the skill shown by her biographers in forming their inductions or deductions from what remains absolutely unknown to us all!

Yet we must not exaggerate. If Thérèse kept her counsel in her own heart, yet sometimes she spoke and often she was observed. She could not hide her frequent and abundant tears.[1] She recognised, moreover, that her sensitiveness was excessive, uncontrolled, if you please. The cause, too, we know. Surely history has the right to take account of these observed facts and of her own avowal.

Yet above all the historian should be a critic. Those who witnessed Thérèse's tears could not see her conscience. Are we then to take at its face value every confession a saint may make of his faults or his sins? We cannot do what is impossible, but some things are within our power. At least, we can doubt. Before we come to our conclusion, let us take time to read the texts, *all* the texts. Whilst we use them and try to understand them, let us remember that no interpretation, however careful and penetrating it may seem to be, can ever take the place of direct and living contact. It is well to doubt even the interpretations that seem to us most obvious. The soul is always a great mystery. When we are dealing with a soul struggling to reach sanctity, we must remember that approved psychological standards are often inadequate, particularly in assigning the true meaning to the language such a soul may employ. How does this apply to the present problem?

In a passage which has not attracted much attention, Thérèse seems to allow us a glimpse into those deep thoughts into which her sister Marie forbore to probe.

"Ah! If God had not lavished so much love and sunshine upon His little Flower, she could never have become

---

[1] Cf. *La Petite Thérèse à l'Abbaye* (op. cit.), p. 38.

acclimatized to this earth. She was still too weak to endure the rains and the storms; she needed warmth, the gentle dews and soft breezes of the spring. These gifts were not lacking to her, even under the snows of her trials." [1]

Everything leads us to think that, standing before the bed of death which was to rob her for ever of her mother's tender care, Thérèse was so overwhelmed with grief that she thought she could no longer live.

If that was her weakness, how well we can understand and sympathize! But if her trouble was the grief—we may well call it " mortal "—which the loss of her mother caused her, what right have we to speak of any loss of harmony between her faculties?

The death of her mother led to the question whether Thérèse would survive. Henceforth this should be clear. There was no question of her falling into any kind of psychological disorder, nor of an upheaval through any moral fault. The problem for Thérèse was not, either at that time or any future time, whether her sorrow would make her so disillusioned with life that she had no longer the will to live.[2] All she wanted to know was whether God willed her to be an earthly flower or a heavenly one. Now that her mother had left her to go to live in heaven, was she to remain to reach maturity in this world which used to seem so beautiful to her when she could constantly cry out: " Mamma "?

---

[1] A. p. 44. These words are confirmed by a later statement which seems to me to remove all doubt from the interpretation I have given above. " Ever since my earliest childhood, I have always thought that the Little Flower would be gathered in its springtime." (A. p. 146).

[2] That is why it is absolutely unpardonable to interpret any of Thérèse's words according to the conceptions of an utterly different philosophy of life. In an article entitled Cendres (La Croix, Feb. 18th, 1947) Père Raoul Plus, S.J., has allowed himself to write: " Here below we are exiles; true happiness is for the life to come. She understands it so clearly that she lets fall a remark which might have come from disillusionment, or from a belated love-affair," (in note [1]: " We are reminded of some of the aphorisms of Mark Twain ") " or from some kind of deliberate pessimism: ' Merely to live we need resignation; death will be an experience of joy.' " No! Thérèse does not " let fall " these words. They are the most profound conviction of her thought and of her whole life. They indicate neither disillusionment, despair nor pessimism, but the unchanging disposition of a saint who is eager for the vision of God.

The reply was to come neither from any strength nor from any weakness in herself, but from God.

We must not think, however, that God's reply was to be communicated to her directly and immediately. That would have been utterly foreign to the normal ways of divine Providence in regard to the future teacher of the "Little Way." It was in her family circle that this little child with the deep thoughts was gradually to learn God's will. On this point, she gives us the clearest information:

> "I could not endure the company of strangers, and I was unable to regain my gaiety except in the bosom of my family. There I continued to be surrounded with the most delicate kindness. My father's heart, already so full of tenderness for me, seemed now to be enriched with a truly maternal love; and both you and Marie became for me the most tender and unselfish of mothers." [1]

Thus, if we understand matters as Thérèse would have us do, if the "little white Flower" was not transplanted to heaven soon after the death of her mother, it was due to her family. We insist on this all the more that it seems to have escaped the notice of that accurate historian, Père Piat, who tells us the story of the Martin family. It is because she found in her father and her elder sisters so adequate a substitute for the love of her mother, that the little orphan was able to acclimatize herself to this world of sad partings. We are then keeping as close as possible to the texts when we conclude that when there first came to Thérèse the supreme question of life or death, her spontaneous answer was an aspiration towards heaven so powerful that, eighteen years later, she thought she could not have remained upon the earth except by the intervention of divine Providence.

But in fact there was such an intervention, and in spite of all, the Little Flower did become acclimatized to this earth and, in the intimacy of her family, regained her gaiety. These three facts are decisive and incontestable. There is

[1] A. p. 44.

another passage of similar import which fills in some details. Three months after Madame Martin's death, the whole family emigrated to Lisieux and took up residence at Les Buissonnets:

> " The whole house seemed delightful to me. There was a large upper window from which the view extended for miles, an English garden in front of the house and another large garden at the back. All this gave fresh delight to my childish imagination. This bright and cheerful house was, indeed, the scene of much quiet happiness and of many precious family memories which will ever remain with me. Elsewhere, as I have said above, I felt that I was in exile, I used to weep and to remember that I had now lost my mother. There, my little heart expanded and I smiled at life once again." [1]

What more can we ask for? Two points are now absolutely certain. During the period that followed immediately upon the first great sorrow Thérèse experienced, the nature of her emotions depended primarily upon her surroundings. When she was at home, she experienced the healing action of kindness and love. True joy and quiet gaiety gave her comfort and allowed her heart to expand. Now that she had moved away from Alençon, and with so much love and tenderness surrounding her, she could forget she was an orphan. It was when she was away from the family circle that the sad truth was always being brought to her memory. Whether people sympathised with her, or seemed to overlook her, whether her little companions spoke of their love for their mothers or whether she saw the caresses they received, it brought back to her mind the sense of her loss and caused the tears to flow anew.

Is this to be called psychological upheaval or weakness? Far from it. Given her loss, such manifestations of grief were perfectly normal. When a child cries because she has lost her mother, what right has psychology or morality to reproach her as unbalanced? Only one far advanced in the

---

[1] A. p. 45.

spiritual life might urge her to rise superior to her grief—
and this was Thérèse's attitude at the time when she was
writing her memories.

It is not for us to take up such a position. We have
to take things as they actually occurred. This poor child
was so deeply grieved at her mother's death that, not on
account of any organic or psychic disturbance, but with her
reason so early in life enlightened by faith she wondered
whether her life was to be continued on earth. When she
was at home, her wound began to be healed by the love and
tenderness she received, peace and joy returned to her and
she thought God would have her live.

When she was with strangers, even the most tactful, she
was always being reminded of her loss, her wound was
re-opened, she thought of heaven, she knew she was in exile
and the poor orphaned child began to weep. People were
surprised. She herself was distressed at it and wished she
could overcome it. Later on she blamed herself for being
hypersensitive.

By all means let her think so. But we need have no
hesitation in saying that this outward expression of her deep
sorrow seems rather to derive from her concentration of
thought, so unusual at such age. It shows clearly that
the faculties that were predominant in this soul were the
very highest.

For, by the death-bed of her mother, she did not shed
many tears, but experienced deep emotions of which she
would not speak to anyone. They were concerned with the
most serious and urgent problem of her life, and so with the
efforts this " little flower " of heaven had to make to adapt
herself to the new conditions of her life on earth. They
demanded all the clearness of vision and strength of will
that she could have at such an early age.

When she was amongst those who tactfully refrained
from questioning her and were, as she instinctively felt, in
the fullest sympathy with her thoughts, she experienced
calm, harmony, peace and joy. When she was surrounded
by people who seemed to demand that she should adapt
herself to this place of exile and make it her home, then

it was that she felt bruised and crushed, and then it was that her tears fell.

Owing to her deep wound of sorrow, Thérèse's interior life, after her mother's death, was profoundly different from what it was before, and from what it was later to become, under the action of God's special grace. But is that the same as saying that we must recognise in her a psychic upheaval which released her emotions from the control of her reason and her will?

No, for the very reason that her wound was not the occasion of any such disorder or other pathological trouble. Her sorrow threw her back upon herself and revealed to her her own deepest thoughts. It perhaps made her feel that she was born for heaven rather than for the earth. She was glad, indeed, to be consoled in her sorrow, and yet it was always at the back of her mind, so that as soon as the happy distractions of family life ceased, it caused the tears again to flow.

Her " weakness," then, was that she allowed the tears to come when she was in the presence of strangers who knew nothing of her deep thoughts. If they had been able to read her soul, they would surely have seen that her bursts of grief were the counterpart of a self-mastery that was truly remarkable. For this tiny child was able to hold in her mind, silent and reserved, the deep thoughts of her opening consciousness, thoughts of life, of death and of eternity.

It is true, however, that there did come to this child a new principle of unrest, though it was radically different from the kind of unrest that hitherto has always been diagnosed. It was an unrest that had its cause from above.

This is no paradox. Whether or not we be right in our interpretation of the deep thoughts that came to the child by her mother's bed of death, it is quite clear that soon after this terrible shock there began a very rapid evolution which led—in the beginning of October, 1882, that is to say, four years and a quarter before her " conversion " of Christmas—to a decision which demanded all Thérèse's wisdom, all her experience, her strength and all the clarity of her mind. All this is perfectly certain, and we have only to be guided by the texts to be preserved from any possible mistake.

Hardly had she begun her life at Les Buissonnets than Thérèse felt called to an intimate interior life of meditation and contemplation. On the flower-covered river banks of the Touques, in a secret corner of her room, a little later on at the Abbey, the little exile received from God a special grace of prayer which showed her more clearly the rapid passage of time, the uncertainty of life, the ravishing and unique beauty of heaven, and inspired her with an ever-growing love of God, an eager desire to avoid every fault and to raise her heart continuously to Jesus her Beloved.[1]

It was a call to contemplation. We must place its beginnings in her fifth or at latest in her sixth year and it went on developing without intermission. She yielded to it unreservedly. It was this call that taught her that not even the tenderest affections of earth must distort her judgment upon the radical insufficiency of all created things. Even the most beautiful religious festivals could not suffice her, though she found, young as she was, the greatest delight in reading the *Imitation*.

This attitude towards the beauties of nature and even of the Liturgy,[2] cannot be attributed to her wounded heart and to the grief that was always ready to rise to the surface, for that would be to take no account of this special call of grace and of the effects it cannot fail to produce in a well-disposed subject, *viz.,* detachment from outward things and a deepening of the interior life.

In fact, if Thérèse had not been influenced early in life by this call to contemplation, she would have found the fullest satisfaction in the beauties of nature which she always loved so deeply, and in the family circle at Les Buissonnets where everyone was intent on pleasing her.

We must insist on this important point. Thérèse's answer

---

[1] *A.* pp. 46-47-72.
[2] As it is by Canon Moreau, *op. cit.* p. 108.

to divine grace has nothing to do with her " sadness." It comes, not from her emotions, but from her judgment. If earth appeared sad to this much-loved child, it was because she knew it was a place of exile. If its delights, dear to her as they were, could not satisfy her, it was because her soul had need of heaven.

Thus a few months, perhaps a few weeks, after her mother's death, she became more detached from earth and more desirous of heaven. The beginning of these aspirations must certainly be assigned to those " deep thoughts " of which she spoke to no one. From this moment there was a growing disaccord between the external conditions of her life and her deepest aspirations. It was the cause of tension and suffering.

In this sense, no doubt, we may speak of a certain loss of harmony in Thérèse's soul. It went on increasing until by God's grace she obtained the helps she needed for the accomplishment of her desires and was placed in surroundings more in accordance with her spiritual needs and more favourable to her aspirations towards her Beloved.

Between her coming to Lisieux and the development of her wonderful love of the Holy Eucharist, there are four or five significant episodes of which we must briefly treat.

When she was five and a half, she first saw the sea. She speaks of her " deep impression " at the sight of the limitless expanse. Was it an impression of vague romance, ready to dissolve into melancholy and tears? Not at all. It was a vivid emotion, but at once it was translated into sublime thoughts. In this spectacle which might have overwhelmed her with its magnificence, she finds only reasons to think of the grandeur and omnipotence of God. In the ray of light which flashes to her eyes, with the help of Pauline she recognizes a symbol of grace. When she has received this lesson, she does not lose herself in idle *rêverie*. She makes a concrete resolution of supreme generosit—nevery to allow her heart to wander áway " from Jesus' sight, so that it may sail peacefully and without delay towards the shores of heaven." [1]

A child who, at this age, is capable of this double reaction, is not one in whom sensibility masters intelligence and will. She is already responsive to the things of God and always ready to raise her heart to Him. Her only desire is to adopt the most efficacious means to reach as soon as possible her heavenly home.

On May 13th, 1880, Céline made her first Communion. It was Pauline who, for several weeks, had been preparing her. She had exhorted her to begin a new life. Thérèse was only seven and was not allowed to assist at all the instructions, but she listened to all she could and took it to herself. She was not allowed yet to make her first Communion, but who was to stop her consecrating the four years she yet had to wait, to trying to get herself ready? She was distressed that she had to wait so long.

Like Céline, she too resolved to begin a new life. For her this meant that she tried to multiply what, even before the death of her mother, she called her " practices "—in other words her sacrifices [2]—and to direct them specifically towards the Holy Eucharist.

Four years before she was admitted to the Holy Table, Thérèse already lived by the Holy Eucharist to such an extent that Céline's first Communion was " as a prelude " to her own. She tells us that on this happy day she received the richest graces and that she ever looked back to it as one of the most precious memories of her life. [3]

All these graces, however, were none too strong to enable her to face her next trial. A little more than two years later, her " little mother " left her to enter the Carmel.

This time the whole edifice of her life seemed to have collapsed into ruins. It was not merely that she was deeply grieved. The very support that alone had made life here below possible to her was now suddenly taken away from her. If she had succeeded in acclimatizing herself to the earth, it was due to the warmth and tenderness with which she was surrounded. Pauline had been her mother and her teacher. Together they had planned to go away by themselves to a far-off desert. And now Pauline had gone—but alone!

Thérèse's anguish was inexpressible. Her tears flowed. Was her sensitiveness now reasserting itself?

For a day, perhaps; but on the morrow light came back to her mind and with it the inner problem that her mother's death had so cruelly set before her:

> "How can I express the anguish of my heart? In an instant life appeared to me in all its reality—filled with continual sufferings and partings—and I shed most bitter tears. At that time I did not yet know the joy of suffering: I was weak, so weak, indeed, that I look on it as a great grace to have been able to endure, without dying, a trial that seemed to be so far above my strength." [1]

For the second time, this child had lost the chief support of her life, or, as we might say if she did not already live so intensely for God, her sole reason for remaining in this world. If she had felt no pain, if she had shed no tears, she would indeed have been insensible.

But yet the reason for her tears is not merely the separation, it is the truth which it exemplifies.

So then, since a child may lose her mother, since a girl may lose her elder sister, just as necessary to her as a mother, life is made up of sufferings and partings. That is the truth. What then can a poor child of nine years old do, who now has suffered a second great shock of grief, save suffer, weep, and perhaps die?

Her cure would come when she could learn to look at suffering in such a light that it could be changed into joy. But Thérèse was not yet aware of this aspect of suffering. Her grief was sudden and overwhelming, whilst she was weak. Her strength was sufficient for the ordinary events

---

[1] A. p. 59.

of life, but here had come a separation so cruel that it threatened her very life itself. She felt unable to face it.

Later on, when she had passed through the dangerous crisis, she attributed her victory to the special intervention of grace. Of this, however, she was not conscious at the time. All that she could realise was the gap between the powers of her soul and the demands of so painful a situation. What she discovered was her weakness.

Here then we undoubtedly have, if not psychic disturbances, at least a danger of such disturbance, of disorder or perhaps loss of her mental balance. Now she had experienced a second most severe shock, and the danger was that she might no longer be able to survive in her shattered environment. But if we have to recognise the danger as it really was, we have also to study the development of the crisis and its ultimate resolution. Both are equally admirable.

The development is twofold. First, Pauline explains to her little sister what is this Carmel which is to separate them. Thereupon, Thérèse reflects, and begins to see that Carmel is for her too. Here is the desert in which she wanted to hide, here is the object at which, more or less vaguely, she has been aiming, since that far-off time, when at the age of two she used to repeat to herself: " And I too will be a nun." There can be no further doubt: God is calling her. In this newly-found certainty, she recovers peace, great peace.[1]

The resolution of the crisis consists in this, that first Pauline, and then the Mother Prioress of the Carmel are favourable to her unexpected decision. Thérèse was in deadly earnest.

The whole episode is thoroughly characteristic of Thérèse. Into the course of a life which a happy environment had enabled a stricken child to accept and to direct more and more consciously towards God, a cruel new grief had come. Everything seemed lost. The tears fell. But as it was the news of Pauline's departure that brought the sorrow, so it was Pauline herself who was able to assuage it. Then

---

[1] A. pp. 59 and 36.

upon this suffering which detached Thérèse still further from all that she could love on earth, was quickly engrafted a new grace. It was a grace that demanded of her much reflection, a grace which led her to a decision which, in view of her tender years and affectionate disposition, we can only regard as heroic.

Thus, for the second time, a crisis in her life is the prelude to a fresh advance towards the summits of perfection. The tears of October, 1882, lead directly to one of the most reasonable, yet one of the boldest decisions that the lives of the saints can show.

Now we must follow Thérèse to the Abbey. There also, there especially, her tears continued to fall. Why?

Several plausible explanations have been suggested which I shall have the opportunity of considering elsewhere. Here it would take too much space to enumerate them, still more to discuss them. Here I would but ask you to try to imagine her feelings when, after such sorrows and such deep thoughts and decisions, she was harassed by the thousand and one puerile duties of school life, when her heart, so deeply filled with God, had now to distract itself with insipid books or essays, with trivial games and similar childish things.

If we would try to imagine what she suffered, we may consider the scene which one of her companions, now a nun in a hospital at Rouen, has kindly described for me. She was coming out of the class where the lesson had been on venial sin. Big tears fell from her eyes. Her face was distorted. According to this eye-witness she looked the *Mater Dolorosa* in miniature.

" Madame," said one of the pupils, " Thérèse is crying."

" It is because she understands how much venial sin offends the good God. How much more mortal sin! And you, children, so easily fall into sin! "

The Reverend Mother who recalled to me this scene—so deeply engraven in her memory—added: " This scene opened my mind to an understanding of supernatural things and made me realise the difference between the two classes of sins." [1]

This happened before Thérèse's first Communion. An anecdote of this kind reveals to us her inmost soul and at the same time indicates one of the causes of her suffering and tears at the Abbey. It had nothing to do with the condition of her faculties, but arose from her precocious realisation of the malice of sin and her compassion for the sufferings of Our Lord. In face of the agonising problems of sin, in face of the Crucifix, Thérèse suffered, and not being able to find any balm of consolation, she wept. Was this weakness or psychic disorder?

Her tears were holy and blessed. They prepared her for her progress to greater heights of holiness and in good time for her oblation to the merciful love of God for the salvation of all mankind.

Still more significant was the terrible trial which, from March 25th to May 13th, 1885, from Easter to Whitsuntide, threatened so gravely both her life and her reason. She was by this time quite sure of her vocation. There can be no doubt that her attack came from the devil and her final cure from Our Blessed Lady. [2]

Perhaps, however, the threefold lesson which, from our present point of view, these events teach, has not been noticed. What is important for us now is whether they strengthen or weaken the general opinion of the child's loss of balance.

The illness attacked her violently. Sometimes the poor girl suffered from violent shivering, or from convulsions, or from a depression so deep that "she seemed like an idiot." [3] She seemed almost always delirious, and suffered from fearful hallucinations. [4]

---

[1] A similar incident is related in *La petite Thérèse à l'Abbaye*, p. 25: "Have you still the Crucifix of the fourth class before which Thérèse used to shed tears of grief whilst the mistress used to speak of venial sin? Her little face was disfigured by grief, at the thought of the agony sin brought upon Our Saviour."

[2] *A.* p. 66: Mgr. Laveille (*op. cit.* p. 110).   [3] *A.* p. 64.

[4] *A.* p. 64. The convulsions have disappeared from Thérèse's reminiscences, but they are proved by the witnesses at the process for beatification, Sœur Marie, Sœur Geneviève, Sœur Françoise-Thérèse, and particularly Mme. La Neèle, who

This illness was surely enough to cause a mental disturbance, if it did not already exist; and if it did, to heighten it or even to lead to insanity. But, though we must admit that we have not enough information to come to a decision upon the nature of this illness, yet what we do know shows conclusively that neither before nor after it did Thérèse suffer from any habitual weakness of intelligence or will.

A first point worth noting is that even when she was delirious or suffering from hallucinations, she never felt that she was losing her reason. On the contrary, she says: "I am sure that I was never for one moment deprived of the use of my reason."[1] She suffered violence, but her mind remained unclouded. Whatever may be the medical verdict upon her condition, the point that here interests us is that she found some comfort in being able to state positively that, although she was reduced to physical impotence, her reason, at least, remained secure.

Clearly, then, her reason was not habitually subject to her sensibility, for if that higher faculty had become weakened, it would never have retained its independence at a critical time like this, when there was such turmoil of mind and body. The truth seems to be that the disease sometimes temporarily hindered Thérèse from acting in a reasonable way, but as soon as the pressure of the attack was relaxed, her mind resumed its normal control of her life.

The miracle of May 13th was not only an answer from heaven to the confident prayers of her father and sisters; it was also the smile of Our Lady on the earnest prayer and tender devotion of her "Little Flower" who had never ceased to implore her aid.

"At times when the pain was less, it was my delight to weave crowns of daisies and forget-me-nots for our Blessed Lady. It was the month of May when nature decked

said: "At the worst period of the illness, there were most violent convulsions during which her body was twisted and contorted in a way which would have been impossible under normal conditions."

[1] A. p. 63.

itself out with the lovely flowers of spring. But the ' Little
Flower ' was drooping and seemed to have withered for
ever! Yet for her, too, there was the benignant sunshine,
for her sun was the miraculous statue of the Queen of
Heaven. Often, very often, the ' Little Flower ' turned
towards this blessed light." [1]

We must go on. When the attacks of her illness were
at their height, though Thérèse kept such control of her
thoughts, her emotions and her actions as was possible, only
too often, however, she felt unable to restrain the agitated
movements of her limbs and the crushing depression of
her mind.

This caused her much distress, even after her miraculous
cure. Indeed, when she had regained her normal condition,
she felt all the more the humiliation of what had gone before.
She could not bear to think of herself as the child whose
words had not been controlled by her thoughts, and whose
actions had not been controlled by her will. She was afraid
she had been untruthful and that she had exaggerated her
illness. [2]

Moreover, as regards the vision itself, the indiscreet
questions that were put to her caused her a similar fear. [3]
From this two-fold distress of mind, even her regular
confessions could not free her. The second trouble was
set at rest only in November, 1887, when she made her
pilgrimage to Our Lady of Victories; the first not until 1888,
with the help of Père Pichon.

To me this distress seems most significant. If she had
habitually compromised with her conscience and not
struggled against her emotions; if she had habitually allowed
herself to be overcome by them and had acted with less
self-control than she might have exercised, then she would

---

[1] A. p. 65.

[2] A. p. 55 and *Unpublished Documents* at Lisieux: " For a long time after my cure,
I believed that I had deliberately pretended to be ill. It was a real martyrdom for
my soul."

[3] A. p. 68: " I imagined I had not told the truth."

not have been so much distressed at the contrast which for these six or seven weeks really did exist between her involuntary actions and her will, and at the possibility that what she *said* she had seen was not actually what she *had* seen. She would simply have felt a little more weak than usual, and more completely overcome. She certainly would not have feared that she had *lied*. The fact, then, of her distress and its continuation seem proof conclusive that, apart from this illness which really did restrain her freedom, Thérèse normally acted with complete sincerity and that neither her reason nor her will were usually subject to the suggestions or the caprice of her sensibility.

This conclusion is strengthened by the fact that from May 1883, to November, 1887, in one respect, and until May, 1888, in the other, Thérèse had to carry on her interior life in spite of such difficulties. " I could not think of myself," she writes, " without a feeling of intense horror." [1] Such inner distress might well have given birth to all kinds of psychic disorder and to the loss of control on the part of her will.

Yet without waiting for the cure of her anxieties (which occurred unexpectedly, in four years' time for the one, in eight years' time for the other), scarcely had the poor child been miraculously cured than she resumed her complete self-control and again began to work, with unflinching ardour, at the realisation of her vocation. A delightful visit to Alençon showed her that she had to make her choice between the attractions of the world and the austerities of the cloister, but there was no weakening of the resolution she had made long since.[2]

She was passionately fond of reading and had a great capacity for hero-worship. She loved the *Imitation,* kept it by her bed-side, and soon knew it by heart. From the beginning of 1884, she began to multiply in a wonderful way her little sacrifices and her acts of love in preparation for her first Communion. This is surely a proof, clear to

---

[1] *A.* p. 68.   [2] *A.* p. 71.

all save those unwilling to see, that her strength of will was completely victorious.

No, Thérèse did not need to wait until her " conversion " in order to learn to live an ordered life of truth and virtue. Far from casting her down, her cruel sufferings helped her spiritual growth.   What happened at Christmas, 1886, was that the Infant Jesus, casting His eyes upon the heroic " Little Flower " whom His mother had long before cured, took pity upon her weakness and clothed her with His armour.

CHAPTER II

The Attraction of Suffering

II.—From May 8th, 1884, to December 25th, 1886.

FOR long years Thérèse had looked forward with ardent desire towards her first Communion, and at last she was admitted to the Holy Table. Her first visit from Our Lord in the Holy Eucharist filled her soul with wonderful graces. But her biographers have been so greatly impressed by the clearly mystical character of the " fusion " then effected, that they have not very carefully studied its exact nature. Thérèse felt especially that thereby her own weakness was made to share in the divine strength. For the chief concern of this unique first communicant was the matter of strength because she had by experience got to know her own weakness.

We should by this time know, and later on we shall know better still, the nature of this weakness. We can now define it as an inability to make at once a completely satisfactory response to the shocks of adversity on the one hand, and the invitations of God's grace on the other. For Thérèse strength meant never to give way to suffering, never to weep and never to hesitate, even for an instant, to accept the call of grace.

But now Jesus has come to her to be Himself her strength. Is that enough for the fulfilment of her desires?

No doubt it would have been, had Thérèse's vocation been an ordinary one. But she was called to such heights of sanctity that her most generous aspirations could not reach the level of God's gracious designs for her. At the very moment of her Communion when she was praying for the strength of God, the Holy Eucharist was creating fresh

needs in her soul of which she had no suspicion. They were
to direct her path towards her destined end in time and
eternity.

Hence the historian places in the second half of 1884,
a new call of divine grace and Thérèse's acceptance of it.
It established a new relation between suffering and her
spiritual life and marked an all-important stage in her ascent
to holiness.

Thérèse was allowed to go to Holy Communion on feast-
days, and each time was prepared by exhortations from her
eldest sister, Marie. One day Marie spoke to her of suffering.
It was no doubt some time after her second Communion
(on Ascension Day, May 22nd, 1884), for what Thérèse
says about it is not related in connection with these first
Communions of such fervent devotion. The *Autobiography*
does not give any more precise indication of time, but we
have only to recall, as Thérèse gives it to us, the matter of
her sister's discourse, to find a confirmation of our
interpretation of the period that began on August 28th, 1877.
It is strange that this important evidence has been overlooked.

Marie in speaking of suffering remarked that God would
no doubt always preserve her little sister from it.[1] These
words to me seem decisive. If, for seven years, Thérèse
had been an habitual cry-baby, of abnormal sensitiveness,
always moaning, always pitying herself, insufferable, and,
from the human point of view, incurable, how could the
closest witness of her daily life possibly predict that God
would always keep her from suffering? She would rather
have encouraged her to hope for deliverance, and to rely
upon Our Lord in the Holy Eucharist to set her free and
allow her to taste happiness. As, however, Marie did nothing
of the kind, but exactly the opposite, it can only be because
Thérèse habitually kept her trials to herself, so successfully
that she gave the impression that she did not know what it
was to suffer. She kept, too, as a deep secret, her very
unusual reaction to her sister's hopeful prophecy.

---

[1] *A.* p. 76: " Once, I remember, she spoke to me of suffering, and said that instead
of making me walk by that path, the good God would no doubt always carry me
as a little child."

The next morning Thérèse went to Holy Communion. During her thanksgiving she remembered her sister's prophecy. At once she received one of those multiple graces which distinguished each successive stage of her spiritual growth. She allows us to see in it four distinct elements and even shows us clearly the order in which they came.[1]

First of all there was a quite unexpected reaction in this child who hitherto had cried so much when suffering came. Now her heart was inflamed with a burning desire to suffer. Then to the emotion of her heart was added a certainty of the mind. Instead of thinking that she would be sheltered from all pain, she felt a deep conviction that God was preparing for her a multitude of crosses. These two reactions were remarkable enough; those that followed were more remarkable still.

The net result of this new desire and this strange certainty was not a start of fright nor a cry from a terrified child; it was a special grace which filled her soul—a grace not only new but quite exceptional. It is strange to notice how now, when she becomes certain that her life is henceforward to conform to the pattern of sorrow that Pauline's departure only just lately had imprinted upon it, it is a flood of consolations which inundates her soul—consolations of such richness, such abundance that she had never known, nor will ever know, the like.

Was not this Our Lord's answer to the prayer she made at her first Communion? Was it not the divine strength which now took possession of this weak child and transformed her into the object of her love?

In truth, this thanksgiving can be compared to a water-shed in Thérèse's spiritual life. It was a crucial date, a decisive

---

[1] A. p. 76: "These words came to my mind after Holy Communion on the following day. Thereupon my heart was inflamed with a burning desire for suffering, and I was inwardly convinced that a great number of crosses were in store for me. At the same time my soul was flooded with consolation so great that all through my life I have never experienced any to equal it. Suffering became attractive to me and I began to find in it entrancing joys, though I did not then appreciate them to the full."

event of mystical character. We cannot understand how writers have treated as homogeneous the long period from 1877 to 1886.

Hitherto Thérèse had suffered with sadness, pain and tears. She had, indeed, with her habitual goodness, tried her best to conform herself to the will of God, but she had never found joy in suffering. She had learnt resignation. In spite of her weakness, she had found, in the loving care her family lavished so generously upon her, strength enough to continue to live where God had willed her to be. The choicest fruit of this time was the peace that came to her with the realisation of her vocation to be a Carmelite.

But now Jesus has come and all is changed!

Suffering is no longer the shock of pain caused by unforeseen separations; it is the cross. The meaning of life is no longer a matter of fallible reasoning from experience, it is an inner certainty coming from God. Strength to meet suffering comes no longer from her own inner resources, nor from external helps, but from His presence in her soul. Lastly, most amazing of all, it is at the very moment when she becomes sure of the coming of the cross, that this young child, so sensitive to pain, far from being frightened, opens her heart to receive most abundant consolations.

She might well have called this great change her "conversion." It was a conversion essentially supernatural, since it was under the influence of the grace bestowed in Holy Communion that Thérèse passed from fear of suffering to a burning desire for the cross. We may see in it the immediate action of God, for the change wrought in her was not in line with human probabilities, nor with her previous dispositions, and it brought with it a triple infusion of light, of burning desire, and of wonderfully consoling graces.

Acceptance on her part, too, was not lacking. Thérèse is at once warned, enlightened and consoled; she does not shrink from the prospect opened up to her. God has suffering in store for her; suffering becomes attractive to her. God offers her the cross; she finds delight where, but yesterday, she found dread.

To be sure, this child now converted to suffering, cannot yet analyse her new impressions. If you had asked her to explain how suffering had now become attractive to her, she would have been in some difficulty to find words to convey her feelings. Yet the fact is there. What before repelled her now attracts her, what used to fill her with pain now gives her joy. She expresses it in a memorable phrase:

" Up to that time, I had suffered without loving suffering. Since then I have felt real love for it." [1]

Let us see where we stand. We have been told that at this date there was nothing to interrupt the uniform course of the years 1877-1886, and that all during this time this child was suffering from a chronic lack of harmony between reason, will and sensibility.

So different is the truth that it suggests a further question. The very fact that this question may be asked shows how frail are the conclusions which hitherto have been accepted.

The question is this. Since, before the end of 1884, Thérèse received the grace of so wonderful a conversion, what more could she receive from the grace of Christmas, 1886, and why did she ascribe her conversion to that later time?

As soon as we make up our mind to take Thérèse as the documents show her to us, we shall find that even before she was twelve, the state of her soul was too complex to be classified under our everyday categories, and yet that we can know it well enough to realise that the conclusions that have been formulated about it need radical revision. It is not enough to observe her external conduct; we must pay the fullest attention to what she tells us.

From her own testimony, then, it is clear that she suddenly received a flood of interior light and grace. Her future was revealed to her. Almighty God shows her that the way of her life will be a veritable way of the cross. Her course is assigned to her. It means suffering. We

---

[1] Unpublished documents at the Carmel.

have no reason to think that she had any knowledge of this kind at an earlier date. Hitherto she had regarded suffering as a reason for not acclimatising herself upon the earth, but for desiring a speedy entry into heaven.

Now that this new light is given her, how does she act—this little child with her " lack of control " and her ready tears? Before coming to a conclusion and deciding into what category she is to be placed, it would have been wiser to study her behaviour.

She is now consecrated to the cross and yields herself to the divine enthusiasm that fills her heart. Henceforward she is attracted to suffering. Far from fleeing from it, she hastens towards it. She is not now governed by imagination, for that would but reveal to her an unending way of the cross, nor by impressionability, for then she would have been overwhelmed by the prospect before her, nor by emotion, for then she could not have restrained her tears. Truly we may say that, under the visitation of God, she is thrown off her balance, and that more and more, but only in the sense we have defined.

She is now under the control of the mighty hand of God and her spiritual powers seem to be raised above their normal functions. Her mind moves no longer upon the level of the things of sense; it finds its delight in the truths of God. Her will, too, has now no other desire than absolute conformity to God's designs.

There is nothing now to feed her imagination or her emotions; nothing which rational psychology would consider adequate to give her balance of mind. Inspired by the Holy Ghost, Thérèse cannot now be put into purely natural categories. If we wish to understand her we must follow her along her unique individual path, and not try to judge her by ordinary standards.

Though she is raised so high, yet she is still far away from the lofty summits to which God is inviting her. Though she has received such wonderful graces, yet, as is always normal in life, she is not exempt from human limitations. Though she has now learnt to love, to value and to desire suffering, yet she remains herself. She may yet be " weak," but the abundant generosity of her heart will help her through the next stage of her journey. Then will come a new grace of " conversion " which will enable her to yield herself without reserve to God and to answer unfailingly to all the demands which her sublime vocation will make upon her.

Though Our Lord promises her suffering, yet He floods her soul with consolations, and she cannot refuse Him her complete loyalty and deepest love. As it is Jesus Himself, her strength and her love, Who will send her the cross, shall she not love the suffering He offers?

She was determined, generously and lovingly, whatever it might cost her, to welcome this most precious gift from Him Whom she loved above all things. Her determination at once raised her to a level so much higher than she had hitherto attained, that we can now understand what she meant by her weakness and why she thought a second conversion necessary.

The desire now engrafted upon her love of suffering was for a love centred upon God alone. With her deep understanding of spiritual things, Thérèse at once translated this formula into words which not only had a deeper emotional content, but were remarkable for their theological accuracy. " To love none save the good God " meant, for her, " to find no joy save in Him." [1]

At this point in her spiritual pilgrimage, this favoured soul, by a supernatural instinct, longed for the *fruition* of God, of which the mediæval mystics wrote. Yet she saw at once that her desire would remain merely a matter of empty words if things of earth could still stir her emotions and comfort her heart.

Therefore, in her thanksgiving a prayer is repeated like a refrain. It is the prayer of the *Imitation,* begging Him Who is sweetness itself to change for her into bitterness all earthly consolations.

[1] *A.* p. 76.

Here again, it is by a mysterious anticipation that such a prayer is placed upon the lips of a child. She confesses that she hardly knew what she was asking. The words seem to be suggested to her.[1] But yet she felt that they were profoundly true and she made them her own at those sacred moments of intimate and undisturbed union with Our Lord in the Holy Eucharist.

We can well understand that she did not fully realise all that her prayer implied, for, in fact, she was asking God to make bitter to her all that had alone enabled her hitherto to support the burden of suffering.

The attractions of Les Buissonnets, her delightful intercourse with her sisters, her love of and pride in her dear father, the beauty of the landscape and its distant views—in a word, all that was not her Beloved—all was to lose for her that strong and living consolation which had given courage and support to her heart, all was to become bitter to her now that her soul was enamoured of the supreme love of God . . . we can go on, because we now know whither this prayer led her . . . so that all these things might become nothing to her and that St. John of the Cross might soon welcome her upon the bare and austere mount of Carmel.

This child called to the highest graces, who had conceived the generous desire of placing her love and her happiness in God alone, added now the prayer which was destined to bring such suffering to her heart and to her whole life. Literally, it was a devastating prayer, for it tended to destroy her most natural sentiments, her most powerful attractions, the supports of heart and mind most necessary, as it would seem, to the development of a normal human life.

This prayer, again, was the beginning of a degree of detachment and thus of a loss of harmony which were to perfect what her earlier trials and the graces of her Holy Communion had already begun. She was now committed

---

[1] A. p. 76: "Often, during my thanksgivings, I used to repeat this passage of the *Imitation*: ' O Jesus, infinite sweetness, change for me into bitterness all earthly consolations.' These words came from my lips almost spontaneously. I used to utter them as a child repeats, without much understanding, the words suggested to him by one he loves."

to swim against the current. Her life was now directed to the heights of perfection. It was she herself who asked for an increase of suffering and trials from Almighty God, who prayed Him to change into a source of bitterness all that normally would be a source of joy.

Here, clearly, Thérèse's prayer went beyond the limits of her spiritual powers. A conflict had to arise between the realization of such a desire—the fruit of an exceptional grace—and the level of her moral strength. This conflict led her, through two years of heroic aspirations and humiliating failures, to the conversion of Christmas, 1886. Then grace completed its work and gave to this brave child who thought herself so weak, the power to check her tears in face of the cross, and to smile, for ever, at pain.

Did Thérèse always remember her courageous prayer? Perhaps not. Yet one fact seems certain and that is that the " One she loved," Who had suggested the prayer to her, was neither slow nor niggardly in answering it.

Though we cannot conceive of her life as following one straight unbroken course, for, like every human life, it had its ups and downs, yet we cannot but notice how, from this moment, occasions seemed to be multiplied when this child who loved God so dearly found that her most innocent joys were indeed transformed into bitterness.

At the Abbey, the good mistresses obliged her to join in games she did not like, and would not allow her to enjoy her favourite pastimes. Her companions met her proffered friendship with coldness and indifference.[1] The retreat before her second Communion became for her a poisoned source of incurable scruples.[2] What she saw of the world in her private lessons showed her clearly " how full it was of self-love "—a confession full of bitterness.[3] When she returned to the Abbey to be admitted to the Children of

---

[1] A. p. 78: "I chose friends. . . My friendship was misunderstood. I felt it keenly. . . Yet God has given me so faithful a heart, that when I love, I love for ever. . . How grateful I am to Our Lord for having allowed me to find nothing but bitterness in earth's friendships. With a heart like mine, I should have been taken prisoner and had my wings clipped."

[2] A. p. 80.   [3] A. p. 82.

Mary, she found that now that Jesus had become her only friend, she could find no other consolation than her silent visits to Him in the Blessed Sacrament.[1]

After this, she still had one precious support and that was her eldest sister Marie. She was " her only oracle," the object of an affection so deep that she could not " live without her dear companionship." But now Marie in her turn leaves her for the Carmel.[2]

We are now in October 1886, with Christmas soon to come. Two years ago Thérèse had asked God, Whom she loved so exclusively, to give her a distaste for all earthly things. During those two years everything had changed for her into a cause of sorrow and a source of tears. She had a great desire for virtue, but the acts of virtue that life demanded of her seemed all of one kind. All of them brought grief to her heart. She was wounded in her instinctive tendencies, in her most legitimate desires, in her deepest affections.

Her immediate reaction was to weep. Then she was conscious of her tears. Even her involuntary faults distressed her. If she felt she had, even unintentionally, given pain to anyone, she could not think of it without weeping. After which, it goes on in a cycle; she weeps for having wept.

Does she realise that these abundant sorrows are a gift from God, Who has taken her at her word and answered her prayer fully?

If she does, she is still too weak to rejoice at it. She says so plainly in an important passage which throws a clear light upon these two years of struggle, of eager efforts to overcome herself, of difficulties and of tears. We have already quoted part of it above. Here it is in full:

> " I have found happiness and joy on this earth, but only in suffering, for I have indeed suffered much. This should be made known to souls. . . Since my first Communion,

---

[1] A. p. 82.   [2] A. p. 83.

since I asked Our Lord to change into bitterness for me all earthly consolations, I had a constant desire for suffering. I did not, however, think of accepting it as joy. That was a grace that was not given me until later on. Up to that time it was like a spark hidden in the ashes, or like the flowers of a tree which in due time are to become fruits. But, as I saw that the flowers were always falling—that is to say, when I saw that I was always giving way to tears when I suffered, I said to myself with sad astonishment: ' Shall I never then advance beyond desires? ' " [1]

What could be clearer? These words are in full agreement with the *Autobiography;* the two texts throw light each on the other and allow us to reach a full understanding of a difficult period which has long been a crux to interpreters.

The period began with this Holy Communion, not long after her first, when Thérèse prayed that she might find nothing but bitterness in earthly consolations. It was an heroic prayer, but her desires never faltered. It was all the more generous in that it expected no compensation in spiritual comfort. She asked simply for suffering, in response to a special grace from God which she had no idea either of debating or interpreting.

From the date of that Holy Communion, Thérèse travelled unswervingly in the direction in which the grace of the Holy Spirit led her. But though she had no thought of drawing back from the path, from the beginning it brought her only surprise and sadness. Her prayer was abundantly answered; sorrow and bitterness came to her in full measure; she fell always into the temptation which her Beloved permitted to beset her generous weakness.

Each time she felt the bitterness of one of these inverted consolations, her virtue reacted too slowly to hinder her tears. She wept, and then, at the thought that once again she had been taken by surprise and overcome by weakness, she felt miserable. Was she never going to reap the fruits of her desires? Her desires had indeed been fulfilled in the sense that sorrows were liberally granted to her, but not

---

[1] *N. V.,* p. 97.

yet in the sense that she could see in them a mark of the special love of her Spouse and could find in them her purest joy.

Such is Thérèse's weakness in this period of transition, and it is, as we must agree, of a very unusual kind. Though Almighty God had given her powerful graces in Holy Communion, yet she had no extraordinary succour, not even the daily reception of the sacrament for which she so much longed. She was but young (from eleven to thirteen years) and her divine Teacher was continuously urging her forward to further progress. The "weakness," then, that resulted was a kind of loneliness, a feeling as of being an exile, and out of place. It disconcerted her and would even have discouraged her, had not her desires been stronger than her difficulties.

The miracle is that, when she saw that all the flowers which she wanted to offer to her Spouse, fell one by one from her hands, she did not abandon her heroic resolution, nor her desire of suffering which brought her always a double crucifixion.[1]

The fault of her biographers is that they have agreed to give the name of weakness to what was, in its final analysis, a magnificent trial of her strength. Jesus, in His design of leading her to the highest sanctity, was making exacting demands upon her. Though she tried with all her heart to correspond to His call, she discovered, young as she was, the essential powerlessness of human nature to rise to such a height as to find perfect joy in the crucifixion of heart arising from God's jealous love.[2]

Now that we have a clearer idea of what preceded, we

---

[1] That is to say, through the suffering itself, and through her distress at its overcoming her.

[2] That is the real state of the case. The most certain evidence assures us that: "No one ever saw her disagreeable, sullen, morose or selfishly hugging her grief. Trials of all sorts fell upon her, moral perplexities, illness, scruples, without making her give way, be it ever so little, to discouragement or negligence. Céline has spoken explicitly upon this point: ' It is important to note that even in her early girlhood's years, she was really strong despite her apparent weakness. This remarkable strength was evident from the fact that her tears never hindered her from fulfilling her duty in even the smallest particulars. So far as I am concerned, I could never find in her at this time any waywardness, any sharp words, any failure in virtue. Her mortification was constant, and extended to the smallest things. It seems to

shall be able to judge of the true meaning of the episode of Christmas. Essentially it is the substitution of divine for human activity and thereby, the passing from defeat to victory.

Her trial was at its height when suddenly freedom came to her. Coming into the house after midnight Mass she was keenly looking forward to the pleasure of unpacking, to the great joy of her beloved father and Céline, the presents stowed away in her shoes. Suddenly there came to her, from him whom she loved most in the world, words that dealt her a hard and unexpected blow. To her great amazement her father showed displeasure and declared that this was the last time that such childishness in a girl now so grown up, could be tolerated.

She was both surprised and deeply pained. His words, Thérèse tells us, pierced her heart. Her eyes filled with tears. But now had come the hour of final victory. What Our Lord in Holy Communion had once inspired her to desire and to ask for, what all her efforts had hitherto failed to attain, was now given to her. She checked her tears in spite of her bitter pain, and she found strength to meet the unexpected trial with joy and to appear before the others "as if she were as happy as a queen." [1]

" Conversion " she calls it, and this time it is true. Literally, she has regained possession of her own soul. Hitherto she had indeed desired and prayed for suffering, but when it came it caused her veritable torture. Now, by the all-powerful grace of Christ, she was raised up to a level where she could not only bear her cross, but love to bear it.

After years of incessant and unavailing struggle, Thérèse was now possessed of this supernatural strength.

That, to me, is the lesson to be drawn from the texts. My critics may perhaps say that I have gone beyond them and that I have tried to make Thérèse greater than her own evidence will permit.

---

me that she never let pass any opportunity for offering sacrifices to God.' " (Piat, *op. cit*. p. 282). This testimony warns us not to be misled about her " weakness." Cf. the excellent remarks of Père Moreau, *op. cit.* p. 133.

[1] *A.* p. 87.

So far am I from wishing to do so, that I will at once make my possible critics a present of the argument that seems to me to suggest most strongly anything that they can find in the *Autobiography*.

When Thérèse declares that on this Christmas night she recovered the fortitude that she had lost when she was four and a half, does she not give us a proof that there was no question of any new problem in her life, but only of regaining the happiness that characterized her before her mother's death? When she tells us that " the source of her tears was dried up " does she not show unmistakably that the only question was whether she could manage to keep back her tears when there was no real occasion for them?

An affirmative answer seems to be supported by a passage in her unpublished recollections[1] in which, referring to this grace, she speaks of ten years of unavailing efforts. This seems to connect immediately the grace of Christmas with her grief as a tiny child. It establishes for the whole period that homogeneous character which I have just been combating.

The consequence seems beyond doubt. As the struggle of the first years of the decade can only have concerned her excessive proneness to tears, so the grace of Christmas can only have been a divine intervention by which, almost miraculously, the source of her tears was dried up and her vocation thus assured.

The case seems very strong. In fact, however, it conflicts with documents that throw light upon the interior life of our saint between 1877 and 1886. The biographers who have been content with the interpretation which, at first sight, she puts forward, seem to have given their attention only to the texts which treat of the beginning and end of this long evolution, unless it be that they know of no others.

With the documents at our disposal, the only conclusion at which we can arrive is the one we have already expounded.

True it is that Thérèse speaks only of the drying of her tears, her reason being that this external sign of her many

---

[1] At the Carmel of Lisieux.

sorrows did in fact remain constant during the whole period, but the sorrows themselves were of very different kinds. If we would know in what Thérèse's " weakness " consisted, it is the nature of the different sorrows that we must study.

True it is also that the girl " converted " in 1886, thanks Jesus for restoring to her the strength of soul which she lost in 1877, but that is not the same as to assert that the strength she received in 1886 was no greater than what she had lost as a child of four. What she really means is that she received by God's grace on this Christmas night the strength she needed to cope with the trials of her adolescence, just as the happy disposition of the tiny child kept away tears in the sunlit days when she still had a mother.

The task which, during ten years, Thérèse failed to accomplish, was one the nature of which was constantly changing. If on Christmas night she had received no more than the strength she possessed at the age of four, under the sudden and unexpected grief that wounded her heart she could certainly not have kept back a flood of tears, still less could she have entered upon the course where henceforward she was to " run as a giant."

The " conversion " of Christmas was proportioned to the demands of grace upon her soul, but that soul had been in continuous progress for ten years. It was now to be raised to those lofty heights where its purification through suffering would be complete.

The texts clearly show that this great grace was all-important in Thérèse's spiritual life and in determining her attitude to suffering. If we were to yield to the temptation to simplify it or to mutilate it, we should utterly distort her picture.

Let us go back to the text. It is so simple and artless that it has imposed upon many a hasty reader. For many, the immediately obvious sense is sufficient: the grace of Christmas is the unhoped-for cure of an excessive sensitiveness, and nothing more. In reality when we take into account all the details contained in the simple, unadorned story, when we rely on Thérèse herself rather than upon the abstract formulæ which the biographers copy from one another, we shall find that the whole matter is not so simple as has been assumed. Yet we can hardly fail to see its true meaning.

To understand that grace of Christmas exactly as Thérèse received and understood it, we must first of all assign to Our Lord the place which she assigns to Him in her narrative. He it is Who takes the initiative in the whole affair. His rôle is not merely unique; it is sovereign. Thérèse's conviction is that Jesus " in an instant " accomplished what all her efforts during the long years had been quite incapable of accomplishing.

Yet the historians have been unwilling to take the word of the only witness who was qualified to speak. They cannot resist the temptation to soften down the contrast that was so clear to Thérèse, and to assign to her a merit of which she was utterly unaware. Some have pointed out the instantaneous character of the victory and ascribed it to a supreme effort of her will " to conquer her sensitiveness," prepared for by ten years of previous efforts.[1] Others have dissected the narration and have shown, phrase by phrase, how it was Thérèse herself who gained, by her correspondence indeed with grace, a whole series of victories.[2]

These explanations, favourable as they are to Thérèse, are in formal contradiction to her own statements and to the obvious implications of her text. In her " conversion " there was, properly speaking, no positive action on her part, only her " good will."

---

[1] Cf. P. Moreau, *op. cit.* p. 135. (See above, p. 42.)

[2] Cf. *Ami du clergé*, Feb. 6th, 1947, p. 95: " But let us make no mistake. Thérèse clings to the grace that is offered, and it is by her prompt correspondence with it that she wins her triumph. ' Keeping back my tears,' she says. ' There is her first victory.' ' I came quickly downstairs to the dining-room.' There is the second, all the more praiseworthy because of her promptitude in self-mastery. ' Stifling the beatings of my heart,' for a child so sensitive must indeed have been deeply stirred by emotion, ' I drew out all my presents with joy, seeming to be as happy as a queen.' There we see her complete victory, a brilliant victory won by the soul of a child." The only fault in this analysis is that though it seems to be complete, it is in fact partial. In a problem of this kind, the greatest care must be taken to leave no element unconsidered. But when we study the *whole* context we find that this analysis deals only with human efforts isolated from their divine principle. If there was a series of victories gained that night by Thérèse, it is because *the victory* was not hers, but Our Lord's.

We are ready to acknowledge at the outset that her narrative does not at once yield its full meaning nor force its readers to adopt one only possible interpretation. We have only to read it to the end to find, in its last lines, a vast perspective opening out before us, out of all proportion to the trivial anecdote to which alone, as a rule, writers have paid attention. We may hesitate to connect the two. Yet we may overcome our hesitation if we follow the text carefully, for then we shall find that the whole scene takes upon itself new dimensions and we shall at length realise that there really did take place a " conversion."

As we read the story in the autobiography, we are surprised at the disproportion between the conclusion and what seems to be the essential part of the incident. Yet we can interpret the whole and understand its true connection, if we will compare the last lines with those that precede the narrative. If we will do this, we shall find our horizon enlarged, and realise that it is a mistake to limit the generous, many-sided action of God to one single effect.

Before we go on to prove our point, there is one fact that from the outset is quite certain. It is that if we arbitrarily assert that Thérèse's earlier unsuccessful efforts produced the sudden transformation, we are contradicting her own statement. Her efforts may in some way have prepared for her victory, but they were powerless, in the full sense of the term, to merit it.

The interpreters all seem to insist on the efforts of her will, whereas she speaks of the action of God's grace. We must study the text closely to decide between Thérèse and her interpreters.

The latter have it in common that they identify the action of Our Lord with this isolated incident at Les Buissonnets. That action, which Thérèse declares to have been alone able to cure her, they restrict to the keeping back of her tears, her quick descent of the stairs to win her victory, the immediate changing of her emotion of grief to triumphant joy, a joy that not only radiated from her countenance, but communicated itself to others. It is to this three-fold victory that they would reduce the whole of God's intervention.

That being their view, it is easy for them to dilate upon the rights of Thérèse's free-will, and her efficacious preparations for the grace in the way of human effort.

But if there is one thing certain, it is that these are not the things Thérèse has in view. Biographers have confused what she has clearly distinguished. The capital fact is this: when Thérèse received the shock which Céline was afraid she could not bear, she was *already* changed.

The fact is clear, for when Céline advised her to wait until she had mastered her emotion, she replied that no delay was necessary. Why? Was it because she felt that at this moment a change was taking place in her and that Jesus was strengthening her heart? Not at all. It was because, as she tells us: " Thérèse *was no longer* the same . . . Jesus *had changed* her heart." [1] Fidelity to Thérèse's text, therefore, demands that we should conceive the events of that memorable night in their due order, for that alone will lead us to a correct interpretation of the " conversion." It is clear, then, that the grace for which Thérèse thanks Our Lord was not given her at the moment of her Christmas victory. It includes it; it explains it; but it is anterior to it and of far wider compass.

When, then, was it given and what was its nature?

Perhaps the second question is easier to answer than the first. If we take the text as a whole and study it in the light of her unpublished reminiscences, we shall find that she recounts four graces that she received on this night. Together they changed her spiritual life so completely that from this time she considers that her true happiness began.

The autobiography enumerates the strength of her will that could now face the most agonizing trials; fraternal charity in winning souls for Jesus; the virtue of constant self-forgetfulness. The reminiscences add a fourth: " a great desire to work for the conversion of sinners." [2]

---

[1] *A.* p. 87 (my italics).   [2] Documents at Carmel.

Can we imagine a more complete conversion, a more wonderful answer to earnest prayer, a preparation more suited to the vocation of which henceforth Thérèse becomes more and more aware? Hitherto, she prayed, under the inspiration of a will, other than her own, that all earthly consolation might be turned for her into bitterness. Yet every time her prayer was heard, her heart was filled with sadness. Now, her will has become so strong that she can master her emotions and smile at her sorrows.

Hitherto, she was intensely preoccupied with her own soul and used her best efforts to adorn it with all possible virtues. Now, she is turned towards her neighbour, and invited to forget herself in order to work for the conversion of sinners.

What a wonderful change and, at the same time, what a great reward! To me it is quite clear: it is on this Christmas night that Thérèse's characteristic spiritual life takes its beginning. She was now completely self-controlled; she could rejoice in suffering; her self-denial was heroic and her apostolic zeal was particularly concerned with the salvation of sinners.

All this was a supernatural state to which she had long before been invited, and was now raised in a moment by the immediate action of Almighty God Himself. Such was, in its fulness, the grace Thérèse recognised as the beginning of her complete conversion. We must accept her word that it was in no way the result of her own efforts. Nothing in herself could lay a claim to it; nothing even was a preparation for it, taken in its fulness.

There can be no mistake about it. One only of the elements of this fourfold grace was in the line of her desires and her efforts, namely strength of soul. The other three were entirely new and unforeseen. No efforts went to their gaining, no auto-suggestion; they were a free gift from Our Lord.

We need not hesitate to repeat it, for Thérèse herself has asserted it. It was Jesus Who changed " into torrents of light " the darkness of this poor little soul struggling with a destiny beyond its powers. It was Jesus Who, Himself having " become small and weak for love of us," made her " strong and courageous." And if He brought her to such perfection, it was not through the development of potentialities she already possessed, or by strengthening virtues she had already acquired, it was solely by making her share in His riches, and by placing " His weapons " in her hands.

Further, Thérèse is convinced that Our Lord made no special demand upon her. He was satisfied with her " good will." He it was Who had done everything. In the case of the Apostles He had at least commanded that they should cast their net. For Thérèse He cast it Himself. If Thérèse became a " fisher of souls," it was because Our Lord, without waiting until she should have the strength herself to do it, had taken the net and dragged it in filled with fish.[1] It was He Who offered to Thérèse the souls she was to save.

Beyond all doubt we are here in presence of the direct act of God. In anticipation of the graces of " the lift," Our Lord bends low over this child and prepares her to become His spouse. He Himself bestows upon her all the graces necessary for her soul, so that, in so far as any such preparation was within her powers, she might become worthy to prepare herself for such a sublime union.

At what moment did this " conversion " take place? One thing is certain. It cannot be assigned to the moment in which her biographers have placed it, or rather, what they consider to be her Christmas grace. Since it is a question of Our Lord's exclusive action, obviously she could not confuse it with her own acts. When she had to restrain her tears, come down the stairs, unpack her toys, smile and spread joy around her, her own " good will " was utterly insufficient. What was needed was a complete gift of herself, and as this pre-supposed a complete " conversion," it follows that it must already have taken place. We may hold this conclusion as certain. The scene at Les Buissonnets did not constitute the grace of Christmas, but brought it into action.

---

[1] A. p. 87.

A fact that we now know, suggests a further inference. Thérèse did not only attend midnight Mass that Christmas, but also she went to Holy Communion. Her unpublished notes speak of it in noteworthy terms; they recall her "happiness in receiving the strong and omnipotent God." Surely these epithets are most significant. Why should Thérèse apply them to Our Lord in the Holy Eucharist unless she wished to emphasise that it was at the moment of His union with her that she received the privilege of sharing in quite a new way in His strength and power? She is convinced that Jesus placed His weapons in her hands and it is in this communication of strength that she sees her Christmas grace. May we not suppose that it was precisely at the moment of Holy Communion, or during her thanksgiving, that there took place that transformation by which Thérèse was "converted" finally and for ever?

The text is not absolutely decisive, but the order of events and Thérèse's own words all point to this conclusion. The young girl who went home to Les Buissonnets after the midnight Mass, was already strong enough to support without flinching a most cruel and unexpected blow. All that had intervened since her Holy Communion was the walk home in company with her beloved father and Céline. The fact that she does not speak of this fateful Communion may perhaps be attributed to her modesty.

After a long series of wearying efforts on Thérèse's part, comes now suddenly God's action which at length assures her victory. She is henceforward raised to a new level. She has now been miraculously given strength to be true to her aspirations and inspired ideals. Now she is ready to go forward triumphantly to the fulfilment of her vocation of intense love of God and of souls.

In speaking of her new strength and her unique vocation, we have laid down the conditions of her happiness. Now that she has the strength to smile at all her sufferings, are we to say that she enjoys happiness without any pain? Or is it rather that, for the future, suffering itself will be happiness to her?

CHAPTER III

The Novitiate of Suffering

III.—From January, 1887, to February, 1893.

THE time is at hand when God will have more to teach her. She is about to have a new experience which we would be tempted to call a new " conversion," were it not that Thérèse herself does not here use the word and that we must not overwork it.

Seven months after the grace of Christmas, our little " convert," now deliberately shaping her course for Carmel, sees the Cross suddenly raised up before her. This time it is the Cross, the true Cross, not a mere personal suffering which her Catholic education has taught her to regard as a cross, not merely an intimate invisible cross which it would be her duty to bear bravely and cheerfully in her inmost heart. Nor was it the great majestic Crucifix before which her tears flowed at the Abbey or that which as a novice she would embrace in the courtyard of the Carmel.

It was the true, the unique Cross, the Cross upon which Christ Whom she loved with all her heart, was extended. It was this Cross which suddenly revealed to her eyes the divine Hand " pierced and bleeding " which was extended towards her and towards sinners. Her eyes fell upon this hand. One single glance was enough to break her heart. Her piercing grief was the beginning of a fresh stage in her spiritual history. It marked this soul for ever with the seal of co-redemption.[1]

Thérèse was delicately sensitive to the inspirations of grace, and at the picture of the divine Redeemer Who shed His blood for the salvation of sinners she began to suffer

---

[1] A. pp. 87-88.

not only more deeply than she had ever suffered before, but as perhaps few had ever suffered. For her emotions before the Crucifix were very far from being similar to those of even the most generous Catholics.

Her grief, as it is described in her autobiography, was neither compassion for the innocent Victim, nor compunction mingled with horror for sin, nor scandal before the deep mystery of justice and iniquity, nor indignation at man's fearful ingratitude in response to God's love, still less terror at what too many writers still call the Father's anger and His punishment of His Son, nor even an inner inspiration to undertake heroic works of penance in reparation.

The sight of the Cross brought none of these possible reactions to Thérèse's mind. Yet what it did bring was based on the soundest theology and a most true theory of the redemption. But as her theology was concrete and living, so was her theory vivid and personal. The understanding that it gives her of the tragedy of Calvary is so acute, so real, that it makes her take her place beneath the Cross and assume an office which henceforth she will ever claim as her own.

What arrests her attention and causes her such deep distress is to see the Precious Blood of Jesus Christ flowing down, with no one troubling to gather It up; but what gives its special character to her emotion and determines her future line of action is that this prodigality on the part of Our Lord, which meets with no response on men's part, is explained by a word uttered from the Cross by Our Lord, which ceaselessly resounds in her heart: " I thirst."

How wonderfully the divine Teacher leads this young child. His graces inspire and direct her. They follow one another in rapid succession, each bringing her to a higher stage of holiness.

In seven months, the child " converted " at Christmas, has now been brought to Calvary. Before, the weakness of the Babe of Bethlehem endowed her with His strength and illumined the dark night in which she was so painfully stumbling. Now, Our Lord from the Cross utters the word which explains the sight that gives her so much grief, and lifts the darkness of Calvary for her who is now to be espoused to Him for the redemption of sinners.   In a single instant He reveals to her the hidden secret of His sufferings and invites her to share in His work by a vocation to a universal apostolate.

Momentous was the invitation given, on this Sunday in July, 1887, to a soul still so frail.   Once again in His condescension the Creator awaits the *fiat* of His creature. In the secrecy of this child's heart a drama is being enacted which may well affect the eternal destiny of millions of souls.

The ultimate reason for Our Lord's suffering is that He lacks those who will bring Him consolation by their active co-operation with Him.   It will be their task to make His Passion efficacious by bringing sinners to be cleansed in the Precious Blood that has been shed for them.   All else is a misunderstanding of Our Saviour's intentions.

There was no such misunderstanding on Thérèse's part. Her spiritual genius, her generosity shine out in her response. She already begins to foreshadow the bold confidence by which she will later offer herself as a victim to God's merciful love, and at once prepares to take unhesitatingly the place that is offered to her beneath the Cross.

Since Christmas she had made her resolution to forget herself in order to practise charity, and now she freely delivers her heart over to the torture of hearing Our Lord whispering incessantly to her: " I thirst!   Give Me to drink." She tries by every means in her power to assuage this thirst and to win souls for Him.   She feels " this burning thirst " growing unceasingly in her own soul.   It becomes " her most delightful reward " because it involves " an exchange of love " between her Crucified Saviour and herself whose only purpose in life now is to co-operate in the redemption.[1]

She means to consecrate herself unreservedly to this task and her fidelity will be unfailing.   On Sunday, August 1st, 1897, she looked back to this grace and spoke of it to Mère Agnès.   Neither of them felt the slightest distress concerning

---

[1] *A.* p. 89.

the manner in which she had carried out the resolution of
ten years previously:

> " Oh! I will not allow this Precious Blood to be wasted!
> I will pass my life in gathering it up for the good of souls." [1]

After July, 1887, the Cross entered deeply into Thérèse's
daily life, not so much to inspire in her compassion with
the Passion of Our Lord, as to obtain for her a quasi-sacerdotal
vocation, by placing her, like a mediatrix of salvation,
between the souls whom she had to bring to Him, and Him
Whom she had to console by their means.

The manner in which Thérèse conceived her task of media-
tion helps much to explain the contemplative vocation of
one who was so evidently called to an apostolate of
immeasurable greatness. It was not her office to go in person
to sinners in order to win them by direct contact and lead
them to Our Lord as to One external to herself. Her task
was utterly different.

It was to pour upon souls " the divine dew of salvation "
in a purely spiritual manner, all the time remaining
intimately united to Our Lord Whose voice never ceased
to resound within her heart, and offering to Him, upon this
same inner altar, all the souls whom she could save.

The incident of Pranzini shows us clearly her method.
She knew well that in such a matter she personally was
powerless, and therefore she offered for his redemption " the
infinite merits of Our Lord and the treasures of Holy Church,"
that is to say, in the concrete, the holy Sacrifice of the Mass
and the most fervent prayers of her heart.

Thus her way opened out rapidly before her. The shock
of a new grief had revealed to her a knowledge of Our
Saviour's designs. Did there result from this any modification
in her conception of suffering and in the welcome which
she was henceforward to give to the Cross?

The texts at our disposal do not allow us to answer this

---

[1] N. V. p. 99.

question with certainty. It looks as if the grace of July, 1887, was a clearly defined illumination of Thérèse's soul which had no other purpose than to develop in her a burning apostolic zeal which was part of her love for Christ Himself.

Obviously such a grace would tend to deepen her understanding of suffering and to increase her readiness to accept it, but as we have no express declaration on her part, we prefer not to reconstruct her spiritual history by means of probabilities.

We do know, however, that when this rare grace came to her, she was already attracted to suffering and filled with an intense desire for heaven. This was owing to an influence of which we are now well assured and the importance of which we can hardly exaggerate.

At the very time when Christ Crucified made Himself her teacher, Thérèse was reading with great delight a certain spiritual book. She never concealed the fact that she owed a great deal to it, and yet it has taken the historians half a century to become acquainted with its nature and its merits. It was the conferences of the Abbé Arminjou. It "filled her soul with a happiness that was not of this earth." [1] She admired it so much that she copied out several passages which corresponded, in a particularly happy way, to the problems of her mind and to the desires which were raising her soul more and more towards heaven.

About a month before the grace of that Sunday in July, she read, admired, transcribed, and dated with her own hand, upon four pages of manuscript,[2] a very important passage from the seventh conference: "On Eternal Happiness and the Supernatural Vision of God." It is this passage she had in mind when in 1895 she wrote in her *Autobiography*:

"I used to meditate upon all that God has prepared for those who love Him; and seeing how these eternal rewards were out of all proportion to the petty sacrifices of this life, I resolved to love, to love Jesus passionately, to give Him numberless tokens of my affection whilst I was still able to do so." [3]

[1] A. p. 90.   [2] At the Carmel of Lisieux.   [3] A. p. 90.

Such an avowal helps us to understand better the eagerness with which Thérèse tried to quench the thirst of her Crucified Lord, and the passage to which she refers throws much light upon the spirit of her apostolic zeal and its relation to suffering.

In the lines I have already quoted,[1] the eloquent preacher of Chambéry reached a level of sublime pathos as he painted, soberly but powerfully, the contrasted pictures of the sufferings of the saints and their eternal rewards. He represented the saints as heroes of unlimited charity who, not content with offering in homage to God the unreserved gift of their leisure, " would have wished to have . . . a heart in their breast that could be consumed a thousand times over by the fires of love; a thousand lives that they could deliver to martyrdom, as perpetually renewed sacrifices." And as God is a " grateful " God, He can repay the gift of themselves that the saints have made to Him only " by giving Himself to them without limit or restriction." He experiences a sort of lyrical satisfaction in seeing that at length the hour of His intervention has come, and cannot restrain Himself from crying out, when He sees before Him this army of heroes entering on their reward: " *Now, it is My turn.*"

These striking words, indicating God's repayment of a debt of gratitude and His communication to His elect of His own divine nature, sank so deeply into Thérèse's soul, that, with the " I thirst " of Calvary and the " Give Me to drink " of Jacob's Well, they became the chief inspirations of her interior life, the stimuli to her acts of generosity, the express motive for her eagerness to welcome and even to seek for suffering. With Céline she repeated the words again and again at the attic window; she comes back to them often in unpublished writings in which she gives free expression to her thoughts.

Once she had made this discovery, she had the key to the enigma which the inevitable sufferings of life offer to all men and particularly to the faithful servants of God.

[1] *Supra,* p. 64

Henceforth there were in her eyes two phases in human life, the earthly phase and the heavenly phase. The second is where Almighty God wills to prepare man's reward, for God's " turn " begins only with heaven. The first is given to man that he may multiply his acts of fidelity to God, his sacrifices, his tears, to such a degree that when the due time comes, God may justly in His own manner, pay him back what He owes, crying out: *Now, it is My turn.*

The only question is whether we realise this truth and are ready to accept the means He offers us to prepare ourselves for our eternal reward, *viz.*, suffering.

A little later, on Monday, July 23rd, 1888, when she had been three months in the Carmel, and was now fifteen and a half, Thérèse explained the matter to Céline. In doing so she could not omit the central idea of the salvation of souls:

> " Céline, fear nothing: He is not far away, He is very close to us. He looks towards us; He *begs* from us our sorrow, our anguish. . . He needs it for souls, for our souls. He wants to give us so wonderful a reward; His designs for us are so magnificent! But how can He say: ' It is My turn! ' if our turn has not first come; if we have given nothing to Him? Ah! It costs Him much to give us the bread of affliction, but He knows that it is the only means of preparing us to know Him as He knows Himself, and to become ourselves as gods. Our soul is, indeed, great and our destiny glorious." [1]

Henceforward, then, Thérèse's programme in life was, for love of Jesus crucified, to devote herself entirely to the salvation of souls and to welcome all the trials and disappointments of this life of exile as precious opportunities for winning the rich rewards of God in eternal life.

The graces of the Holy Eucharist and her own determination to correspond unreservedly to every call from God had transformed this sensitive little child into one so sure of possessing the key to eternal happiness that every suffering here below had now become dear to her.

---

[1] Letter xxxiii.   Date rectified: cf. *A.* p. 333.

But there has been much misunderstanding in this matter, for which the attractive manner of her writing has been a contributory cause. She did not write to draw up a list of her sorrows, but to sing the mercies of God towards her soul. Thus it comes about that often she masks under gracious language and pleasing imagery, events that other writers might well have described as pathetic or even tragic.

The charm of Thérèse's style is a subtle combination of such delicate qualities that it is difficult to analyse. One of its most obvious characteristics is its exquisite simplicity. She is a privileged child who has received wonderful graces from God. Though with the light of the Holy Ghost she ranges familiarly amongst the mysteries of the supernatural life and of eternal happiness, yet she knows well her own limitations and offers her homage for them to the infinite wisdom of her Creator. She eagerly accepts Our Lord's invitation to intimate friendship and especially delights in the condescension by which He became a Child. In the Infant Jesus she loves everything, even His caprices.

There is another side to the picture. Her spontaneous imagery has sometimes been mistaken for puerility and childishness. How strange! In reality at the very moment when she was comparing herself to a little ball in the little hand of the little Jesus, she was overcoming one of the most insidious dangers, and gaining one of the greatest victories of her spiritual history. At this very time her correspondence to grace was raising her, once for all, to the level of perfect conformity with the holy Will of God.

In proof, it will be enough to read what she writes in her autobiography concerning her journey to Rome, but certain unpublished information to which I have had access will help us to understand the full bearing of this testing-time. So far as I can see, it has never yet been assigned its rightful position in Thérèse's path to holiness.

Thérèse was now sure of her vocation, and on May 29th, 1887, she obtained from her high-minded father permission to leave him and the world and to enter the Carmel the

following Christmas, the anniversary of her "conversion." [1]
There followed five months of determined effort to overcome
various unforeseen obstacles which at length, on November
20th, brought her to the feet of Leo XIII. What was the
state of her mind when this girl, not yet fifteen years old,
approached the Holy Father?

Before we can answer, we must briefly recall the details
of her efforts and her attempts. The six months were
filled with deep, if unexpressed, sorrows. Before she spoke
to her father she had to endure many interior trials. [2] When
she had gained his consent, she had to approach her uncle,
M. Guérin, of whom she was always a little afraid. From the
beginning the good man was utterly opposed to the idea. It
was not that he doubted the vocation of his niece, but he
considered it to be quite impossible to allow a girl of fifteen
to enter Carmel. It would be, he said firmly yet not
unkindly, "a veritable public scandal." [3]

To overcome this obstacle would need a miracle. Thérèse
could not expect such a miracle and had no resource but
prayer. Her grief, however, was so deep that she could
not hide it from her sister Pauline. The latter wrote to
M. Guérin a week later to inform him of the position. The
letter shows us the seriousness of Thérèse's trial and lets us
understand her intentions when she set out for Rome. We
quote a portion of it:

> "Thérèse, the poor little Benjamin, was so pale, so sad,
> so unhappy this morning that I had to make her tell me
> the cause. . . A whole week of agony. . . Her eyes were
> so sad and tearful that I was sure there was something more
> than an ordinary childish sorrow. 'What is the matter?
> Are you ill?' 'No, Pauline, but I have never suffered
> such pain. If it goes on, I shall die of grief. I see quite
> well that my uncle is waiting for a miracle, but Our Lord
> is not going to work a miracle for me. People say that
> to enter the Carmel at fifteen is extraordinary. It is most

---

[1] A. p. 94: "I was resolved to enter Carmel at the very time when, the previous
year, I had received my grace of conversion."

[2] A. p. 93-94.

[3] Letter xi, to Sœur Agnès (Saturday, October 8th, 1887).

unfortunate that it should seem extraordinary, but it seems
to me that God never asks for impossibilities, and yet He
is asking this from me. . . O, Pauline, I have no hope
but in prayer. I pray and pray, you know how fervently!
Every day I say to Our Lord: ' O my God, Thou art
all-powerful and my uncle is always obedient to Thy voice.
When he receives Thee into his heart, tell him that Thou
art asking for me without delay. I have been greatly tried
this week; I have suffered much; give me a ray of hope. . .
The journey to Rome will be burdensome to me so long
as Thou dost not assure me it is my *wedding journey*. . .
O Jesus, take me at Christmas.' " [1]

Wonderful to relate, the first part of this prayer was
answered. M. Guérin was soon convinced, for his heart
was touched. Then began Thérèse's struggles with the
ecclesiastical authorities.

The superior of the Carmel refused permission, though at
the same time he said he would yield if such were the wish
of the bishop. Mgr. Hugonin, however, would not consent,
but he did not try to dissuade her from appealing to the Pope.

In obedience, then, to the call of Jesus, Thérèse had to
set out for Rome. But Sœur Agnès told her that she was to
ask nothing of the Pope. It was a very hard trial of obedience.
Though she did not wish to fail in docility, she could not
help saying to herself that she could get no answer if she
put no question. Yet she resigned herself absolutely to the
Will of God and felt sure that He would in due time give
some signs of His good pleasure. [2]

The sign was not long in coming. She received it at
Rome on November 14th. Sœur Agnès had changed her
mind. She wrote that Mère Gonzague and Mère Geneviève
advised her to speak if she so desired. Mère Geneviève
had said: " Do not forbid her, above all, to speak to the
Holy Father."

Not only did Sœur Agnès remove her prohibition, but
whilst she continued to tell her little sister to do nothing

---

[1] Unpublished letter of October, 1887, at the Carmel of Lisieux.
[2] See the letter in the next note.

but what Jesus inspired her to do, she did not hesitate to
tell her how to act and to suggest the words she should use.
First, she was not to be overawed by those who stood
around and might hear what she said. Then she was to begin
thus: " Holy Father, I have a great favour to ask." She was
not to fear to repeat her words, if the Holy Father paid no
attention to them. Then she was to make her request in
these words: " Most Holy Father, in honour of your jubilee,
give me permission to enter the Carmel at the age of fifteen."

Sœur Agnès even foresaw the possibility of a reply that
was discouraging or negative. Then Thérèse was to say
to herself that it was Jesus Himself to Whom she was
speaking; she was to make her appeal again and again,
remembering the perseverance of the Chananean woman.
Sœur Agnès then adds the encouraging item of news that
the formidable Canon Delatroëtte has confessed that if the
Holy Father says " Yes," Thérèse will enter without difficulty.

When Thérèse had received this letter she knew that if
occasion offered, she was not to hesitate to speak. She had
to await her opportunity.[1]

Now comes the decisive moment. Thérèse is on her
knees at the feet of the Sovereign Pontiff. Is she going
to speak?

As if to contradict the sign received from Lisieux,
M. Révérony has just forbidden anyone to speak to the Pope.
But Thérèse thinks she is supported by a higher authority
and this, too, is Céline's view.

She speaks then. In humble deference to the instructions
of her " little mother," she addresses the Vicar of Christ in

---

[1] Unpublished letters at Carmel, one from Sœur Agnès, one from Thérèse to
Sœur Agnès (November 14th, 1887): (Since the bishop is unwilling, the only
means I have left is to speak to the Pope, but of course I must find an opportunity. . .
If only you knew what pleasure and comfort I have received from what you say in
the letter I received at Loreto!) and one on the same day to her aunt, Madame
Guérin (I do not know how I shall manage to speak to the Pope. Indeed, if God
were not taking charge of the whole business, I do not know what I should do. But
I have such great confidence in Him that He cannot abandon me: I put everything
in His hands. We do not yet know the day of the audience. It appears that the
Holy Father, in order to speak to everyone, passes in front of the faithful, but I
do not think he stops. Yet in spite of all I am determined to speak to him, for even
before Pauline wrote to me, I was thinking of it; but I said to myself that if God
willed it, He would give me a sign). Piat, op. cit. p. 315, quotes part of this letter.

the exact words she has been told to use. The Pope does not seem unfavourable, but rather very thoughtful. But then the mention of " superiors " spoils the picture. Thérèse however, remembers what her most determined opponent has said and ventures to add: " Most Holy Father, if you say ' Yes ' . . ."

As the Chananean woman had importuned Our Lord, so did Thérèse wish to importune His Vicar. She would have told him all that was in her heart, her convictions and her reasons for hope, *viz.*, the permission of her father, the call of Christ which gave her no rest, the agreement of the Carmel of Lisieux as to her vocation. . .

But the Pope had no time to listen to a long speech. Yet, if he would not discuss the matter, neither would he give a decision. He put the matter in the hands of God, and the noble guard at once removed the tearful supplicant.

It was quite time. It was a strange scene. If it had continued it might have become scandalous. One venerable priest went back to the group he was conducting to tell them that they must no on account act in the way Thérèse had acted. . .

From the external standpoint, Thérèse had failed utterly. She had tried to follow the urgent call of God, and to follow strictly the advice she had been given, but she had experienced a repulse; she had made an exhibition of herself; she had hopelessly compromised her cause. Was it not the end? Was not her life spoiled?

It was a bitter conflict, even a tragic one. On the one side were her deepest convictions which she knew to be in correspondence with God's will; on the other, was the Church. She was called by Jesus Himself to co-operate as closely as possible in His work of redemption and she could not conceive it possible for her to do otherwise than take the place in the Church to which He was inviting her. But, as soon as she had tried to obey God's call, she was met by refusal on the part of the Church. She was brave and did not give in. But each new appeal to the ecclesiastical authorities brought her a fresh disappointment.

Now she had come to the end. No fresh appeal was possible. In referring her back to her superiors and then to the will of God, the Pope who, in her eyes, was Jesus living upon earth, had left her in the dark helplessness from which he alone might have drawn her.

In reality, as she was to know later on, the Pope's last words were prophetic.[1] But at the time all that she knew was that she had been repulsed. There seemed to be an insoluble conflict between her holiest aspirations and the reply of the Church. The highest and most sacred authority was hindering her following the call of God.

Could there be a more tragic situation for one who was so sure of her convictions? What was to be done? She might easily have given way either to rebellion or despair.

Had not God taken too literally the prayer of this naïve and over-confident child who loved Him so ardently? It was surely under His inspiration that three years before she had begged Him to change into bitterness for her all earthly consolations. Now indeed bitterness was overflowing in her soul. Had she then tried to find consolation in any earthly good?

All that she had done was to answer, as well as she could, the call of Our Lord. It was He Who had called her; it was He Who had led her to Rome; it was He Who in the person of His Vicar, had suddenly abandoned her.

Further, not content with confounding the hopes of His child, He had abandoned her interiorly. In her heart was not only keen suffering, but a silence that was even worse. At the very time when, in her effort to follow Our Lord's call: "I thirst," she had tried to bind herself for life to the work of redemption and had therefore been bold almost to rashness, Jesus was silent. . .

It was but a short time before when He had urged her on to heroism by making her repeat " with incredible fervour: *Now, it is My turn*."

[1] At Lisieux, her sister Marie was more clear-sighted and hastened to reassure Thérèse. But her hopeful letter arrived too late to hinder Thérèse's suffering from the emotional shock she had sustained. Cf. Piat, *op. cit.* p. 319.

Now that His turn has come, He says nothing. So far as her intentions can go, Thérèse has already sacrificed everything to Him. His Vicar repels her. And He, Who led her to the scene which ended her hopes, now gives no sign. One might think that He was not concerned in the matter. He seems to disappear and leave no sign of His presence.[1]

Interiorly as well as exteriorly, Thérèse was abandoned. Never before had she suffered so deeply. Who could be surprised at her tears when the noble guard removed her?

After receiving such a repulse, many a soul has been for ever estranged from God or from His Church. But it is when she suffers most that Thérèse is most admirable. At this crisis of her life, a false step might have been fatal, but she found her safety and a rapid advance to the most heroic sanctity in unreserved and uncomplaining conformity to even the faintest indications of God's Will.

But now she begins to disconcert the gravity of the theologians by choosing simple illustrations which they are only too ready to declare to be trivial or even puerile. It was at this dramatic moment that the rejected child compared herself to a little ball with which the Infant Jesus plays. Did she mean that she was unconscious and did not know what was happening? She makes her meaning clear when she deliberately offered herself to the Holy Child.

> " . . . as a ball of no value which He could throw to the ground, kick, pierce, leave in a corner or press to His Heart if it should please Him." [2]

This has been laughed at as infantile. One learned writer in her defence has shown that a similar comparison does not lack good authority, the Scripture, Latin poetry. . .[3] But what is the need of this? If the criticism of Thérèse is absurd, apology is superfluous. On the other hand, if

[1] A. p. 115.

[2] A. p. 115.

[3] Annales de S. Thérèse, 1934, p. 75, and Études et documents Thérèsiens, 1934, p. 19, note 1.

Thérèse's expression were in itself indefensible, it would not help to show that there was a verbal coincidence between her metaphor and a scriptural or pagan comparison.[1]

The comparison expresses a sublime truth. She trusts her Spouse implicitly; she unreservedly respects His liberty; she has no thought of questioning, even for a moment, His infallible wisdom or His unfailing love.

Already before her departure for Rome, Thérèse had adopted this metaphor of such pregnant meaning. Already she had accepted all its practical consequences. A week before her great disappointment, she had recalled to Sœur Agnès this fundamental truth:

> " Jesus must get everything ready, so that His little ball will have nothing to do but roll where He wills." [2]

Such is the masterful character some of the biographers describe. The more we study in the concrete this gentle and humble child, the more we may wonder what these good people were thinking of when they were writing about her.

Thérèse resolved to remain absolutely passive under the action of God, whatever it might be, and showed that she had so fully assimilated this doctrine that no surprise, disappointment or sorrow could henceforward move her.

It was this conception and the determination with which she made it the law of her life, that saved her. She might be crushed: it was but Jesus Who was piercing His little ball. To-morrow He would press it to His heart.

---

[1] The verbal agreement, however, hides utterly incompatible doctrines. It would be instructive to make the comparison. When Plautus (Captives, Prol. v. 22) writes: Enimvero Di Nos, Quasi Pilas, Homines Habent, he means that the gods make men their playthings, whilst men can know nothing of their purpose, nor take any initiative in the matter, nor hope for any good to come from these amusements of the immortals, nor retain any kind of control over their own lives. In proportion, it is very much the same with the text quoted from Isaias xxxiii, 18, where the prophet is speaking of a pitiless chastisement. In her excellent book, Une Parole de Dieu, Blanche Morteveille has these words, which are very much to the point: " ' Puerility,' some will say. ' Admirable virtue,' will reply those who have deeply studied the saint's spirituality. She chooses deliberately a naïve expression to express her entry upon the royal path of absolute trust in God, which will lead her very far and very high " (p. 115).

[2] Letter xv, to Sœur Agnès, written in Rome, November 14th, 1887.

Thus, little Thérèse has suddenly been raised to such greatness, that we can but feel the truth of what she writes in her *Autobiography*.

> " At the beginning of my spiritual life, when I was thirteen or fourteen years old, I used to ask myself what there was that I could learn later on, for I used then to think that it would be impossible to get a fuller understanding of perfection." [1]

What, indeed, was lacking to this child who had resolved to yield herself unreservedly to all the desires and even the whims of her Beloved, even when they were utterly unexpected, apparently unreasonable or inexplicable? She looked on her greatest disappointment as an answer to her prayer; she looked on her keenest pain as a revelation of the inmost dispositions of her soul to Him to Whom she fully entrusts every detail of her future.[2] At the bottom of her heart she was conscious of great peace. She ceased not " to hope against all hope," to guard herself against any bitter feeling towards those who had exposed her to such a discomfiture, to maintain control over all her resources, so that she might continue " to struggle and to suffer." [3]

She still had to learn the exact place of the Cross in her life. She had to sacrifice her desire to choose for herself the dates when her wishes were to be realised. She had to retain her sensitiveness to grief, and yet to turn it into pure joy and divine happiness.

Though she was so great, she could grow still greater.[4] Of this further growth we must now briefly note the chief stages, in the Carmel.

---

[1] *A.* p. 132.

[2] *A.* p. 115: "In a word, I wanted to amuse the Infant Jesus and yield myself to His whims. He heard my prayer! In Rome, He pierced His little plaything; no doubt He wanted to see what was inside!"

[3] *A.* p. 119: Thérèse adds: " Yet my confidence was undiminished, and I still hoped to enter on Christmas day."

[4] After thinking for a time that she had reached stability, Thérèse recognized her mistake. After the text quoted above, she adds: " but I very soon realized that the further we advance along this path, the further away we find ourselves from its end. Now I am resigned to seeing myself always imperfect and even find my joy therein."

Very early in her life Thérèse had learnt the value of sacrifices and had begun to practise them for the love of Jesus. Thus she had met the great trials of her adolescence with the fixed resolve to refuse nothing to Him Who had chosen her as His spouse. The reason for this resolve should be noted. Thérèse speaks of it one day to her sister Pauline:

"I should have loved to see you, but it is another sacrifice to offer to Jesus. I will refuse Him *nothing*. Even when I feel sad and lonely on the earth, He always remains to me. Has not St. Teresa said: ' God, by Himself, is enough for us '?"[1]

Her meeting with the Holy Father soon put her conviction to the test. On the very evening of her audience, Thérèse, with a heavy heart, poured out her sorrows to her dear Carmelite sister, now so far away. Yet her faith triumphed over her distress. "Oh! Pauline, now I have no one but God, Him alone." But she was able to assure her, with a conviction the merit of which we can now appreciate, that absolutely nothing was changed in regard to her dispositions towards her dearly-loved Infant Saviour:

"Pauline, I cannot tell you what I felt. I was crushed; I felt that I was abandoned, and then I am so far away. . . As I write this letter my heart is so heavy that I would wish to weep. Yet the good God cannot send me a cross that is beyond my strength. He has given me the courage to bear this trial. Oh! it is a heavy trial, indeed, but, Pauline, I am the *little ball* of the Holy Child. If He wants to break His *toy*, He may do so. Yes, whatever He wills, I will also."[2]

What He wills is that this child, already so wonderfully faithful to Him, should learn to smile heroically even amidst the cruellest sufferings. So far He has only placed her in the novitiate of suffering. Three years were sufficient for Him to bring this most tender and sensitive heart to such a close union with His Will.

[1] Letter xi, October 8th, 1887.
[2] Letter xviii, written November 20th, 1887.

Yet though united, their wills still remained exterior, one to the other. The metaphor Thérèse employs suggests a complete distinction, a duality. On one side, Jesus; on the other, His little ball. What He wills, she does not know. The toy is pierced and makes no resistance, but it does not understand the designs of its Owner. It does not delight in suffering.

But now, in ten years, Jesus is going to change her submission into loving and clear-sighted union with His Will, her passive acceptance into active co-operation with all His designs, her resignation into a unity of purpose, of inspiration and of love.

To this end He is going to employ a simple and direct method, which will be as effective as it will be painful. She has already, at the age of fifteen, offered Him her heart and for His sake has sacrificed what she held most dear; but now He will demand still more, the complete sacrifice of all that she most loves and reverences—her father, her spiritual consolations, the sweetness of His presence—all is taken from her without delay and without reserve.

This child, from the early days when reason first dawned in her soul, had never ceased to aspire eagerly towards her heavenly home and to employ all her energies in winning heaven for repentant sinners. Now, however, first of all He wills her to travel through a dark tunnel where cruel doubts often bring her anguish; then, at the very hour when her dearest wishes seemed now about to be accomplished, He allows her to be tormented for long months by insidious temptations against faith and hope.

She consecrated herself to Him, to be with Him a victim of Redemption; she wanted to devote her whole life, by means of her contemplative vocation, to the needs of the apostolate and of the foreign missions. But He does not preserve her from a most painful malady and from death at an early age.

Thérèse asked for the Cross, and obtained it in rich abundance. It would be truer to say that Jesus offered her a life of complete crucifixion. But by accepting it with all the heroism of her pure love, and even with smiles of joy, she has taught us the most universal and the most useful of all her lessons.

Her religious life held for her so many trials and sufferings, that unless she had entered it without any illusions, she would have been most grievously disappointed.[1] To draw up a full list of what men of the world would call her miscalculations, would lead us too far afield. We can obtain a general idea of her progress in suffering, and we can see opening out before us the royal road of the Cross by which she is henceforth to travel, if we recall merely those which followed immediately upon her victory.

Hardly had she entered into the Carmel, where God Himself had shown her that He wished her to be, than she ceased to hear His voice, to experience His strength, to feel the sweetness of His presence.

Eager to obtain guidance, and yearning for supernatural affection, she found in the Mother Prioress, who represented to her the authority of God Himself, little but severity and lack of understanding.

Then her dearly-loved father, whom she reverenced as a saint, was lost to her more cruelly than if he had died. He was paralysed and unable to come to visit her. His fine intelligence was clouded.

It was the Cross from which she had seen the Blood of our Redemption flowing. She had loved it and now it had become hers. Would it be too heavy for the shoulders of this girl of fifteen?

Her reply is expressed in a cry of joy which, since 1888, has been inscribed upon marble in letters of gold: " Sit Nomen Domini Benedictum "—Blessed be the Name of the Lord.[2] He had not, indeed, deceived the hopes of His supernaturally enlightened spouse. But why precisely is He to be blessed?

Because now Thérèse had learned the true value of suffering.

---

[1] A. p. 122: God in His mercy and goodness preserved me from illusions. I found religious life such as I had imagined it. No sacrifice took me by surprise.
[2] In the chapel of the Carmel, cf. Piat, op. cit. p. 357.

It was in October, 1888, that she wrote these inspired words to Céline:

> " Remember that if God gave us the whole universe with all the treasures it contains, it could not be compared to the very lightest suffering." [1]

The very lightest? What shall we say of the heaviest? Later on when Thérèse painted her coat of arms, she wrote under the words " Our great grace " the date on which her father entered the home of the " Bon Sauveur " at Caen. Shortly before she had explained in the clearest way this paradox, which comes as a shock to so many sensitive readers:

> " Later on, in heaven, it will be our delight to look back upon these dark days of our exile. Yes, the three years of our dear father's martyrdom seem to me the richest and the most fruitful of our lives. I would not exchange them for the most sublime ecstasies; and my heart, conscious of this invaluable gift, cries out in gratitude: ' Blessed be Thou, O my God, for the graces of those years that we have passed in misfortune.' O my dear Mother, though our cross was bitter, how precious and sweet it was, for from our hearts came nothing but aspirations of love and gratitude! No longer did we walk, we ran, we flew in the paths of perfection." [2]

Heavy or light, suffering is always a mark of God's special love: He gives the Cross only to His chosen friends.[3] Such were these generous young girls whose aims were henceforward expressed in the words: " To save souls and to pray for priests."

As this was their purpose, there could be no doubt about the means:

---

[1] Letter xl, October 20th, 1888.

[2] *A.* p. 130.

[3] Letter xlii, to Madame Guérin, November 18th, 1888: " I should be only too willing, for your feast, to relieve you of all your grief and to take upon myself all your sufferings. Just now I was asking this of Him Whose Heart was then beating close to my own. But I felt at the same time that His most precious gift was suffering and that He reserved it to His chosen friends. I realized that Jesus loved my dear aunt too much to take away her cross."

> " When a man wants to reach an end, he must take the
> necessary means. Now that Jesus had made me understand
> that He would give me souls through the Cross, the more
> the Cross fell to my lot, the more my attraction to suffering
> increased. For five years this way was mine, but I alone
> knew it. That was the very flower I wanted to offer to
> Jesus, a hidden flower which would breathe out its perfume
> only in heaven." [1]

She could not have entered upon this mystical path with
clearer sight, nor could she have welcomed the supreme law
of Redemption with greater generosity. For five years she
travelled alone upon this secret way of sorrow—a veritable
way of the Cross.

These years cover the period 1888 to 1893, from her entry
into the Carmel until the election of Pauline as Prioress.
These are the years in her life of which we know least, for
during them she wrote less than at any other period. Perhaps
however, of all her years they were the most precious in
the sight of God. They were years of silent suffering which
none suspected, yet perhaps then she laboured more for God
than at any other time. It was a period of increasing
incorporation with Christ, and of preparation for perfect
union with Him.

Her manner of spiritual combat, and even the general
character of her spiritual life at this period, have been
described in a phrase that has been widely quoted: " The
asceticism of littleness." [2]

---

[1] *A.* p. 123.

[2] Cf. H. Petitot, *op. cit.* (p. 3). The writer contrasts " older asceticism or
asceticism of greatness " with the " asceticism of Sœur Thérèse or asceticism of
littleness." His purpose is quite legitimate; the development of his idea gives
occasion to many just observations and to remarks that are very much to the point.
But yet I must be allowed to regret the choice of his two terms, for it is based on
an ambiguity, it develops it in a most dangerous manner, and leads inevitably to
sentences like the following: " The great merit, the special genius, the providential
mission, of the little St. Thérèse of the Infant Jesus was to have seen more clearly
than ever before that all-too-neglected sanctity of littleness which overtakes the
sanctity of greatness " (p. 17).
This seems to me disastrous, for Thérèse's great merit was not at all to have
distinguished a sanctity of greatness from a sanctity of littleness, in order to build
up, so to say, the latter at the side of the former, but rather to have understood

We must be allowed to doubt whether this is a very happy phrase. It is easy to see the reasons which have suggested it. Thérèse made no attempt to practise fearful bodily austerities, but said that she tried to heap up little acts of the little virtues. Yet if it is carefully analysed, the formula will be found regrettable rather than acceptable. It has several defects. The least is that it suggests, if it does not assert, the lower value of Thérèse's manner of mortification; the greatest is to use the terms "greatness" and "littleness" in a false sense. We cannot call "great" what is on a human scale, exterior and material, and "little" what is purely spiritual and therefore beyond our standards of measurement.

How can we apply the term "little" to a series of operations in which the body has little place, but the soul exercises the highest virtues and the utmost self-denial, by clinging to every indication of God's Will, and identifying itself with it in untiring generosity?

The truth is that Thérèse's asceticism is of the purest, the highest, the greatest kind. It involves painful, continuous and prompt mortification of even praiseworthy desires and sentiments; it involves accepting the holy and most wise Will of God as the supreme standard of judgment and action, even—or especially, as Thérèse in her unfailing wisdom would say—when it crucifies us.

Was Pascal deceived in his scale of values? Did St. John of the Cross, after his successive searching purifications, arrive at something little?

Thérèse's asceticism, so simple and so spiritual in its methods, is one of unmixed greatness. It is based upon the

that the achievements of a certain kind of bodily asceticism, violent and easily degenerating into Pharisaism, far from constituting holiness or even contributing to it, were calculated to hinder it and to promote self-love. It was not then a "sanctity of greatness" to which she was opposed, but a sanctity which imagined it could find its basis or its strength in strenuous human efforts, that is to say, to put it bluntly, in a parody of sanctity or in an absence of sanctity. That Thérèse was so clear on this point was proof, especially in her special circumstances, of her clear judgment. When all is said and done, even for the man who practises the most violent austerities, there is no true sanctity unless he walks by the little way of St. Thérèse, that is, by the way of humble charity. The chapter: "Littleness and Greatness" contains much that is excellent, but it does not emphasise the supreme value of the spiritual element in mortification.

most powerful and most elevated conceptions, and it is rich in aphorisms, so vivid and direct as almost to be disconcerting in a child so humble and docile:

> "Each new suffering, each anguish of the heart, is like a light breeze of Spring which carries to Jesus the perfume of His lily. Then with a loving smile He at once gets ready some fresh bitterness and fills the chalice to the brim, for He knows that the more His lily grows in love, the more she must also grow in suffering. What a great privilege to receive from Jesus so great a sorrow! Eternity itself will not be long enough to thank Him. He loads us with His favours, as He loaded the greatest of the saints." [1]
>
> "We must offer our sufferings to Jesus to save souls. Poor souls! They have fewer graces than we have and yet Our Lord shed all His Blood for their salvation and He wills that their eternal happiness should depend upon a single aspiration of our hearts. How wonderful a mystery! If one sigh can save one soul, how many souls may be saved by sufferings like ours! Let us refuse nothing to Jesus." [2]

Her asceticism is one of greatness, because it is on the highest level, it derives from the noblest principles, it is bound up with a most complete understanding of the mystery of the Redemption; lastly, and perhaps most of all, because it is not so much to be conceived of as a punishment, an expiation, a mortification, or something preparatory to a loving union with God, but it is essentially such a loving union and it grows with the growth of love:

> "True love feeds upon sacrifice, and the more the soul denies itself the satisfactions of nature, the more its affections become strong and disinterested." [3]

It is an asceticism of greatness, because it is complete and continuous. Bodily mortifications are necessarily limited

---

[1] Letter lviii, to Céline (here meant by "the lily"), February, 1889, cf. A. p. 334 (date corrected).

[2] Letter lxi, to Céline, March 12th, 1889.

[3] A. p. 175, referring to her dispositions in 1892.

and intermittent; the soul's gift of itself is unreserved and constant:

> " Let us make our life a continual sacrifice, a martyrdom of love in order to console Jesus." [1]

It is an asceticism of greatness, because its character is not only, or chiefly, to cause pain, but to transform the soul. Properly understood, that is to say, in the divine plan, it is the necessary starting point for supernatural progress:

> " Alas! It costs Him much to give us the bread of affliction, but He knows that it is the only means to prepare us ' to know Him as He knows Himself, to become ourselves divine.' What a marvellous destiny! How great is our soul! Let us raise ourselves above all that is transitory and keep right away from the earth. Up there the air is pure." [2]

Of its very nature Thérèse's asceticism is a preparation for our becoming as God Himself.

> " We are greater than the whole universe. One day we shall have, *ourselves,* a share in God's life." [3]

It is in preparation for this day that Thérèse, at the age of sixteen, invites her sister into the Carmel to share her life of trial and suffering. We can understand how Céline regarded her sister as " sanctity itself." What we cannot understand is that an historian should use the word " littleness " to designate a condition of soul of which Pascal would have envied the nobility, the balance and the strength.

But Thérèse far transcends Pascal's deepest thoughts. From the time of her retreat for her clothing, she finds the solution of her double problem, how to be enamoured of

---

[1] Letter lxxiv, to Céline, October 15th, 1889.
[2] Letter xxxii, to Céline, July 23rd, 1888, date corrected (cf. *A.* p. 333).
[3] Letter lviii, to Céline, February 1889 (cf. *A.* p. 335).

the Cross, and at the same time to lose none of her eager desire for happiness.

On January 7th or 8th, 1889, Sœur Marie was much moved at learning this fact. Less than five years earlier she had regarded her little sister as especially privileged by God, in so far as she would always be preserved from suffering. Now, however, she found how much she had been mistaken. Thérèse showed her how she had trodden the path of suffering, but yet found her happiness in it.

Her way was one of universal and absolute detachment. She was content that God alone should know of her sufferings:

> "Why should we seek happiness in earthly things? I can assure you that I have a most ardent desire for happiness, but my poor heart sees that no creature is capable of satisfying it. On the contrary, the more deeply it should drink of the deceitful streams of earthly joys, the more raging would its thirst become. But I know of another stream, in which, if we drink, we shall still have thirst, but a thirst that is not breathless, but on the contrary very pleasing because it has the means of satisfaction. That stream is suffering known to Jesus alone. . . !" [1]

If Thérèse loves "little sacrifices," it is for several reasons, but especially, perhaps, because her own desire for happiness and her longing to quench the thirst of Jesus invite her to approach this stream and to drink there so eagerly that no suffering, however small, may escape her.

Is this littleness or greatness? It is love and self-sacrifice which are always rising to still greater heights of heroism.

The triumph of her greatness was doubtless that she so quickly learned the lesson of the mystery of God's deep and tender love for men.

Under the combined influence of the trial of her father's illness, the counsels of her "little mother," and her more and more profound meditations upon the Passion, Thérèse had not been more than a year at the Carmel when she experienced the need of development. No longer was it

---

[1] Letter lii, to Sœur Marie, January 7th or 8th, 1889.

enough that she should regard herself as the plaything of the Infant Jesus. Now she had to be assimilated to our suffering Saviour Whose wounds revealed to her His agony and His unfathomable love. The revelation pierced her own heart with sorrow.

It was on January 10th, 1889, the day of her clothing, that there appears, in her manuscripts, for the first time, the addition of " the Holy Face," to the name she had first chosen for herself.[1]

A long study would be needed to analyse the motives for this addition and to understand fully its connection with the history of her inner life. But as it certainly does mark a change in that life, it serves to show how insecure is any interpretation which regards the period from Christmas, 1886, until her death as essentially homogeneous.

On the day when Thérèse decided to lengthen her name, she came still nearer to Jesus Crucified. True it is that since July, 1887, she stood in spirit on Calvary; but though it was her aim to strive to distribute the Precious Blood, she was not yet perfectly assimilated to the Divine Victim. Now, however, she meditated unceasingly upon the *Volto Sacro* and found there, together with ever fresh revelations of the inner dispositions of Our Lord, a sufficient explanation of her father's malady, and the model and the support for her own life of suffering and love.

Hitherto she seems to have had no special devotion to the Holy Face, but now it took a central place in her spiritual life. It was an inexhaustible subject of meditation, it was her supreme consolation, and a model ever set for her imitation. Though her earlier love of the Infant Jesus knew no diminution, this later devotion grew to have a special attraction for the young Carmelite. Better than all other instructors, it taught her love and humility.[2]

According to our available information, Thérèse was struck by this lesson of the Holy Face, because she realised its

---

[1] Documents at Lisieux.

[2] *A.* p. 338 and Piat, *op. cit.* (p. 354).

application to the illness of her father.   Already on April 4th,
1889, we read in a letter to Céline:

> " Let us sing in our heart a sweet canticle to our Beloved. . .
> The music of our suffering, united to His Passion, ravishes
> His Heart.   Jesus burns with love for us. . .   See His
> adorable Face; notice how the Eyes are veiled and lowered;
> study His wounds.   Fix your eyes upon His Countenance. . .
> There you will see how He loves us." [1]

But it was not until July 18th, 1890, that Thérèse compared
the humiliation of her father with that of her God:

> " Papa!   Ah!   Céline, I cannot tell you all my thoughts.
> How can we complain when Jesus Himself was looked
> upon as a man struck by God and humiliated? " [2]

No doubt it is possible that Thérèse had this comparison
in mind at an earlier date, but as we must be guided by the
texts rather than by conjectures, we have no right to say
that it was her father's affliction that led to her devotion to
the Holy Face.[3]   So far as our evidence goes, the devotion
came first.

It is none the less true that its application to her father's

---

[1] Letter lxiii.

[2] Letter lxxxviii, to Céline, cf. A. p. 338.

[3] Still less are we entitled to say that before she recalled the image of the Holy
Face, there passed before her mind the memory of the vision she had had in her
childhood of the old man with the veiled face in the garden of Les Buissonnets.
According to Père Piat, op. cit. p. 355: " On the day that M. Martin was struck down,
she lived again, this time in terrible realism, the former scene." He makes the
memory of this vision precede the comforting comparison with the Holy Face:
" Then her horizon widened and the comparison forced itself upon her, irresistibly,
like an obsession, between that father, so good, so holy, walking in silence bent
under his burden, and Him Who was, beyond all, the Just Man, stripped of His
glory, His face swollen, His brow stained with blood, become like unto a leper.
From Thérèse's unpublished reminiscences we can show that this interpretation,
specious as it is, is not true.   In truth, the order of events is the reverse.   First
of all it was the analogy of the Holy Face that came to her mind, and it was only
after some years that the memory of her early vision was unexpectedly revived:
" The vision had a meaning which one day was to be revealed to me.   The day was
long in coming, but after *fourteen years* God Himself drew aside the mysterious veil."
As a little before she says that the vision had occurred fifteen years earlier than the
date at which she is writing, we may conclude that it took place in 1880, and that
it was only in 1894 that she understood its meaning.

illness made the devotion still more precious to Thérèse
and the source of very many sacrifices. She found valuable
lessons in Chapters 53 and 63 of the prophet Isaias, as she
tells Mère Agnès on August 5th, 1897, when she even went
so far as to reduce all her piety to this one devotion:

> " My devotion to the Holy Face or, more truly, all my
> piety, was based on these words of Isaias: There is no
> beauty in Him, nor comeliness: and we have seen Him
> and there was no sightliness. . . Despised and the most
> abject of men, a man of sorrows and acquainted with
> infirmity: and His look was, as it were, hidden and despised,
> whereupon we esteemed Him not. As for myself, I, too,
> wanted to be without comeliness or beauty, alone to tread
> the wine-press, unknown to all creatures." [1]

That this reminiscence is strictly in accordance with the
facts, appears from the letter of July 18th, 1890, to Céline,
for it includes, written out by Thérèse as an appendix, the
two essential passages from these chapters of Isaias, and
formulates the practical conclusion for herself and her sister:

> " Since Jesus trod alone the wine which He gives us
> to drink, in our turn we must not refuse to be clothed
> in blood-stained garments. Let us tread out for Him a
> new wine that will quench His thirst and return Him
> love for love. Ah! Let us not lose a single drop of the
> wine we can offer to Him . . . then looking around Him,[2]
> He will see that we are there to help Him. . . His look
> was, as it were, hidden. . . Céline, so it is to-day, for
> who understands Our Lord's tears? " [3]

We need only a superficial knowledge of Thérèse's life
as a Carmelite to understand how perfectly she kept this
heroic resolution in silence, in the secrecy of her heart,
in intimate union with her Beloved.

With her eyes fixed upon the Holy Face, Thérèse found
unfailing strength to realise, in its perfection, the life's
programme which, at the attic window, had filled her heart,

---

[1] N. V., p. 112.　　　　[2] Isaias lxiii, 5.
[3] Letter lxxxviii, cf. A. p. 338.

and Céline's, with such ardour: " Lord, to suffer and to be despised for Thee! " [1] She speaks of the Holy Face as " her heritage," " the coin given to her to redeem souls," [2] " her native land," " her kingdom of love " where she resolves " to live unknown and alone." [3]

In order to communicate to her novices her burning zeal for the salvation of souls and her intense love of Our Lord, she consecrates them to the Holy Face. [4] When she puts into verse the principles that sustain her life of love, she sings:

> " To live by love, it is to wipe Thy face
> It is for sinners pardon to obtain,"

thus uniting inseparably the love of the Father, the love of Jesus Christ and the love of her neighbour.

We know that these lines, addressed by her to the picture of the Holy Face which she passed on her way to the refectory, made her weep tears of love on the morning of February 26th, 1895. [5] But by this date the period of beginnings was over and the time of full development had come.

---

[1] *Sup.* p. 65.   [2] *A.* p. 451.   [3] *A.* p. 125.

[4] *A.* p. 450. This is a most important text.   The Consecration to the Holy Face was not composed for the novitiate as a whole, but for the three religious who held that title, and who signed thus: " Th. de l'Enf. Jésus et de la Ste. Face; G. de Ste. Th. Marie de la Ste. Face; M. de la Trinité et de la Ste. Face."

[5] That is the date of the poem, cf. *N. V.*, p. 111-112: " On that day, going to the refectory after the examen, (*i.e.*, at 11.7 a.m.) I had composed the verses:

> To live by love, it is to wipe Thy face,
> It is for sinners pardon to obtain.

I repeated them to Our Lord, as I passed His picture, with much love.   Turning my eyes towards it, I shed tears of love."

CHAPTER IV

Peace Through Suffering

IV.—From February 21st, 1893, to her death.

WHEN one of Thérèse's character makes the Holy Face " her native land," important consequences will necessarily follow, especially in regard to her reaction to suffering. We see this clearly with Thérèse, at least from the year 1893.

Before this date, texts are too infrequent to enable us surely to distinguish the various stages through which she must have passed. At this date her interior life obviously undergoes a modification of a nature that history is apt to neglect, but yet is important alike for the historian and the theologian.

Monday, February 20th, 1893, however, might have brought danger or even disaster to her. For five years she had trodden her lonely path, ever advancing, with growing confidence and heroism, along her way of complete self-oblation, following the rule as perfectly as she could and offering as many sacrifices as possible, often most painful ones, upon the invisible altar of her love.

On this day, however, the conditions of her life were suddenly changed. In place of Mère Gonzague, who had trained her with rigour, her sister Pauline, her " little mother," was elected prioress. Almost at once, as an extraordinary mark of esteem and trust, the latter entrusted Thérèse with the formation of the novices. At the same time Thérèse discovered a talent for expressing in verse the thoughts and sentiments on which she had long meditated.

What a change! The danger was that Thérèse would let herself be carried off her feet, would lose the benefits of her long trial, would prefer joy and lack of restraint to

recollection and suffering, in a word, would vulgarize her
spiritual life.

It might have happened to others, but not to Thérèse.
Quite the contrary. Her purification had been too thorough;
her fidelity under her trials had been too clear-sighted and
generous, for a change of superiors to affect her religious
character, or to lead her into relaxation of her ideals or her
practice. In circumstances where others might have found
an occasion for slackness, she saw only reasons for maintaining
or even surpassing her previous efforts.

Such was her constant custom. Her keen sense of
spiritual realities led her to an increase of humble confidence
in her heavenly Father. With the powerful help of grace
she advanced to the level towards which she had for so long
been striving, with such heroic efforts, the level where
suffering, however keen or continuous, became her happiness.

She was glad that God had given to the community so
good a prioress, but for her part she was supernaturally
indifferent to the person in whom was vested the authority
of the divine Lord Whom she obeyed. So detached was she
from all consolation that, of all the nuns, she was the one
who most rarely had recourse to Mère Agnès. In her
responsible charge she saw but a motive for humility, for
trust in God, for prayer and zeal. As to her poetry, that was
written merely out of charity to others. Thus Thérèse
never for one instant relaxed her strivings after the highest
perfection.

We might well ask what more, at this time, she still
had to acquire. She had always desired suffering, and had
grown unceasingly in her understanding of it. From the
time of her entry into the Carmel she had realised that it
was the painful but necessary means for the salvation of
souls, for our growing into the likeness of our Redeemer,
and for our becoming divine. Moreover, she had learned
from Jesus Himself that her vocation was a vocation to
suffering. She had made it her aim to save souls, especially
the souls of priests, and she knew that this involved increasing

suffering on her part. But the more she suffered, the more she wished to suffer:

> "As Jesus had made me understand that He would give me souls by means of the Cross, the more often I met the Cross, the more my love of suffering increased." [1]

Such was her habitual disposition since the time of her entry into Carmel:

> "Since my entry, suffering has stretched out its arms to me and I have embraced it with love." [2]

Was it possible for her to advance beyond this vocation to the Cross, beyond her generosity in accepting it, beyond her understanding of its mystery, beyond her courage in loving what human nature shrinks from and employs every means to ward off?

Yes certainly, for Thérèse did so advance. Her love, for all its eagerness and generosity, had not been hitherto without some sadness. Her understanding of the mystery had not yet taught her what a privilege it is for human nature to be able to suffer. But now she " turned to the Director of directors, and unfolded herself under the shadow of the Cross, having for refreshing dew His tears, His Precious Blood, and for radiant sun His adorable Face " [3] and thus she transcended the limits in which hitherto she had been held. Grace now teaches her to penetrate more deeply into the mystery of suffering. Her soul is enlightened and grows in love and confidence. Not only is the Cross now to be desired for its intrinsic value, whatever may be the pain that accompanies it, but it is a privilege, a happiness and a joy.

It is a privilege, because man alone can suffer as did Jesus, with Him and for the same ends. Angels, pure spirits in the enjoyment of eternal beatitude, are unable to suffer, and envy men their privilege.

It is a happiness, because, being in accordance with the

---

[1] *A.* p. 123.   [2] *A.* p. 123.   [3] *A.* p. 125.

order of our salvation and the adorable Will of God, it brings men into union with the wisdom of God and the designs of His infinite mercy.

It is the highest joy, for it is the triumph of grace that nature should find its highest perfection in that which mortifies it. It is the highest joy when at length the soul finds nothing so sweet and attractive as to do the Will of the Father even when it brings it to crucifixion and death.

From the year 1893, Thérèse began to advance more rapidly until she reached her full development in this deep-seated and radiant joy. Her verses and her prose provide such abundant evidence of the fact that it is difficult to select quotations without giving the impression that we are omitting other equally valuable passages. Yet we must try to choose a few striking expressions of her superhuman serenity.

First, a few lines from a letter to Léonie. They will show that whatever advance Thérèse made in the things of the spirit, she did not lose her prudent realism and her practical commonsense:

> " Little crosses are all our joy: they are more ordinary than the bigger ones and they prepare us to receive these when it is the will of our good Master." [1]

Then, some extracts from her poems. She puts the following prayer upon the lips of St. Joan of Arc, one of her favourite saints because she had the double privilege of martyrdom and of dying for France:

> " The sacrifice I love, the cross is my desire
>   Oh! deign to summon me, full ready now am I
>   O Master, for Thy love to suffer I aspire
>   Jesus, my well-Beloved, for Thee I long to die."

She gave the following counsels to her novice, Sœur Marie-Madeleine, on the day of her profession:

---

[1] Letter cxxvi, August 13th, 1893.

" If bitter pain your life invade,
   Threatening gladness to destroy
Of anguish may delight be made.
   Suffer for God! 'Tis purest joy.

" Then will His tenderness divine
   Each sorrow heal, each memory dim.
Though thorns bestrew your steep incline
   You will not walk, but fly to Him."

The following was a song of thanksgiving, for the intention of Sœur Geneviève:

" Divine Beloved,
   Jesus, bend down to hear
Whom Thou hast hid within Thy Sacred Face.
I come to sing the ineffable grace
   Of having suffered,
Taken the cross to bear.

" For long my lips
   Drank from the cup of grief.
And I have shared the chalice of Thy tears. . .
And understood that suffering's charm endears,
   That by the Cross
Sinners may find relief.

" For by the Cross
   It is my soul, matured
Now to descry, has glimpsed horizons new;
Beneath the rays Thy Sacred Face imbue
   My heart now soars
Towards dreams most fair inured."

This is how she conceives a life of love:

" To live by love is not on earth to rest,
   E'en though on Thabor might our dwelling be;
But 'tis to climb to Calvary's rugged crest,
   Holding the Cross. . our heart's sole treasury.
In realms celestial, joy hath endless sway
   There trial shall no more the spirit prove;
But here below, in anguish deep I pray
      To live by love."

Thus does she define the ecstasy of which she sings when sorrow is changed into joy:

> " All pain, O Lord, becomes delight
>   When loving heart to Thee takes flight."

And this is her description of the joy itself:

> " In the crucible of pain
>   My love to Thee I long to prove.
>   All other joys will I disdain
>   Save immolation for Thy love."

The solution of the theoretical problem and of the practical difficulties aroused by the various sufferings of mankind, not excluding the greatest of all, death, is to take delight in them as in so many proofs of love.

One who suffers for love's sake and to prove his love, dies also to prove his love. Thus death becomes great happiness. Previous sufferings are a preparation for it and are virtually contained in it. Thus it becomes the choicest offering that a spouse of Christ can present to her crucified Lord.

As the rose of Spring sheds its petals one by one, so was Thérèse's life fast ebbing away. Yet her happiness was ever increasing, for by her little sacrifices and the love that inspired them she knew that she was sweetening, for her beloved Spouse, the bitter agony of the Crucifixion.

> " For Thee, O Love divine, I am to die;
>   My Jesus, scarce can I contain my joy.
>   I'll breathe to Thee my love with every sigh
>   Though bitter anguish may my life destroy.
>   I wished, O holy Child, to tread with Thee
>   The humble steps of Thy simplicity.
>   To share Thy dol'rous way to death, I'd fain
>   Walk in Thy steps and sweeten all Thy pain." [1]

[1] *La rose effeuillée* (May, 1897). We can see why Thérèse could not approve of the suggestion of the Rev. Mother who wished her to add a verse upon the restoration of the Rose in the glory of eternal life. Her instinct was sure when she refused to give a conventional ending to a poem which expresses the joy of suffering and death for the Beloved.

But with Thérèse, it is never enough to underline the delicacy of her sentiments, their sublimity or their purity. We have to penetrate deeper and to discover the theological truths that underlie them.

" What happiness! " cries the little Carmelite at the thought of dying for Jesus, the supreme Beauty, and of thus giving Him the supreme proof of her love. Her exclamation of joy is neither exaggerated nor hysterical, but a logical consequence of her deepest convictions. Two remarkable passages throw light upon two complementary aspects of these convictions.

The love which inspires a man to share in the sufferings of Christ Crucified and thus to lessen His torments, can be called angelic. By it he shares in the office of " the angel of the Holy Face," who by his compassion shared in Our Lord's Agony and pleaded with Him for the pardon of sinners:

" To Me in grief and sorrow, angel dear,
    Honour and lowly reverence didst thou show.
To mystic truth, O angel, now give ear:
    All suffering souls, as sisters henceforth know

" In heaven the pain they bore for Me
    Will add its glory to thine own.
The brightness that belongs to thee
    Will add a lustre to their crown."

Yet, magnificent as it is, this idea of a relationship issuing in a communication of heavenly glory is not the ultimate limit of Thérèse's thought. When she speaks not merely of the sufferings of this particular angel, privileged though he was by his close relation to the Cross, but of suffering in general conceived as a proof of love, and of the angels as such, even of those who stand closest to God in heaven, then Thérèse does not hesitate to go much further.

Boldly she inverts the natural relationship of men and angels and considers that man has the advantage in being able to suffer. This original idea, based on sound philosophical and theological grounds, inspired this child of genius with some of her best verses. She makes an angel say:

> " I am lost in my God, and His wonders I see,
>   But for Him I can never know suffering or pain.
> No tears and no blood can I offer to be
>   The pledge of a heart that for Him would be slain.
> The angels above in His purity share,
>   This infinite joy is their lot without end;
> But thou canst be both pure and suffering bear,
>   And thus e'en the Seraph in rapture transcend." [1]

Now at length the transformation of suffering is complete, or rather, it has changed its place in the scale of values. There can be no further doubt, suffering is the most precious treasure that we can possess on our journey to heaven. Even Thérèse herself cannot recall these sublime truths without a feeling of awe and reverence for the wonderful goodness of God:

> " How great the soul must be if it can become the dwelling place of God! Yet the soul of a tiny baby a day old is for Him a paradise of delights. What will it be, then, with us who have struggled and suffered to give delight to our Beloved! " [2]

Even yet she has not reached the limit of her development. Though in her sublime faith, she makes a joy of suffering, a further stage is still possible. We may be quite sure that this soul, invited by the Holy Spirit to the greatest heights of sanctity, will reach this stage.

In fact she does correspond with this final call, but the words in which she speaks of it are so discreet that we might miss her meaning.

It was towards the end of 1895 that she penned these decisive lines. She has not clothed them in the magic of poetry, nor in lyrical form such as distinguishes the last

---

[1] N. V. p. 182 (September 27th, 1897): " Oh no! I am not an angel. Angels cannot suffer, they are not as happy as I."
[2] Letter cxliv, to Céline, July 7th, 1894.

pages of her letter to Sœur Marie. The simplicity of her language serves to hide what might well be uttered in the thunders of the Apocalypse. It is the last word of her wisdom, the most precious pearl that her teaching and her example have to offer us; in its trust it is revolutionary:

> " Now I have no longer any desire, save to love Jesus even unto folly. Yes, love alone attracts me. I no longer desire pain or death, and yet I love them both. Long did I call upon them as messengers of joy. Suffering came to me and I thought I was nearing the shores of heaven. From my earliest years I thought that ' the little flower ' would be culled in its springtime; to-day I leave myself entirely in God's hands. He is my God and I need no other compass. Now the only petition I can make with any fervour is the perfect accomplishment of the will of God in my soul." [1]

In our poor judgment we might have thought that the heights she had already so painfully scaled were the limit of her spiritual progress, but now we see her rise still higher. Raised up, as by the wings of an eagle,[2] she discovers, in its simple perfection, the final secret of heroic sanctity. It is the purest Gospel teaching and henceforth it is the law of her life. Her trials continue to the very end; she is now the victim of holocaust to the merciful love of God, but in her sufferings she finds the most perfect joy.

If we would penetrate, so far as is possible to human understanding, the mystery of this chosen soul, and gain an exact knowledge of her attitude to suffering, we must interpret these quiet and undemonstrative words with the greatest possible care. We venture to say that Almighty God Himself invites us so to do, for by its results we can judge how deeply the fervent and unique prayer they imply touched the very Heart of the Eternal. We must try to understand

---

[1] A. p. 146.

[2] This eagle's wing has not yet appeared in her text, but no doubt it was already in her mind. It had unceasingly sustained her in her life and it will raise the conclusion of her letter to her sister Marie (now the eleventh chapter of the *Autobiography*) to sublime heights.

them thoroughly; then we shall grasp what is meant by the complete unfolding of the " Little Flower."

When, towards the end of 1895, or at the beginning of 1896, Thérèse finished the manuscript she had written for Mère Agnès, and thought that thereby she had finished the story of her inner life, she stated that two desires had been uprooted from her heart. Much might be said about both of them, but one only now concerns us: the desire for suffering.

We are well acquainted with it. We have seen its beginnings at the time of her first Communion, its continuous growth as she began to realise her special vocation and to work for its accomplishment; we have seen how finally this desire for suffering became identical with her desire for happiness. How could she lose such a desire? How could she be content to see it go, and not rather react against what must surely have appeared to her a falling away from perfection? It seems inexplicable, for, after all, her progress in the spiritual life corresponded to the growth of her idea of suffering in precision, richness and sublimity. We have seen how, at length, her desire for suffering seemed to be identical with all that was best in her life. It was a desire to be nailed with Christ to the Cross and to co-operate with Him for the salvation of souls, thus to share in His divine nature and to give Him the supreme proof of love.

We can well understand that she should have desired suffering, but not that she should have thought it preferable to renounce the desire.

Thérèse's solution of the delicate problem comes at an important time in her spiritual history, and is to be very carefully distinguished from two other doctrinal positions with which one might be tempted to confuse it. The matter becomes clear when we remember that to give up the desire for suffering is not the same as to give up affection for suffering. Though Thérèse no longer desires it, she loves it as much as ever. There is no change in her understanding of it, nor in her eagerness to cherish it. But—and the distinction is no mere subtlety, though it is profound—she feels no more drawn to desire it for itself or to seek for its increase or strengthening. She loves it when it is present. She is far from wishing to exclude it from her life or to lessen its intensity. But she does not ask for it when it is absent nor is she distressed when she is deprived of it. She does not now regard it as the supreme criterion of God's favour, and as a sure guarantee of a happy eternity, but as a subordinate good, a good far lower than this other good which even here below can include it and give it all its meaning, *viz.,* love.

What has changed, in this young Carmelite so responsive to grace, is the disposition of her heart, that is to say, from her point of view, the essential element of sanctity.[1] She began by desiring suffering though its real character and its attractions were alike unknown to her. She persevered although she experienced it in all its intensity, and she even found in it " a messenger of joy."

Now, however, a new desire possesses her, of an entirely different character. It is expressed in a comprehensive prayer and a new disposition of soul. It is the only desire she now has, and it takes the place of all her earlier desires, even the two strongest. It is the desire to love Jesus even unto folly. Essentially it is a prayer for the complete fulfilment of the Will of God. The only disposition of her soul that ultimately remains is the complete yielding of herself into the hands of God.[2]

Thus has Thérèse reached her full development of soul. We should note that it is later in date than her act of oblation to the merciful love of God. Its character and merit may be judged by comparison with systems that have their centre in the Cross, like that of Louis Chardon, and, on the other hand, with the classical system of St. John of the Cross.

At the date when Thérèse tells us, without regret, that she no longer possesses the desire for suffering, six or seven

[1] *Infra*, p. 109.
[2] Here the reader will doubtless recognise the untranslatable word *abandon*. Thérèse wrote a poem on the text of St. Augustine: " *L'abandon* is the delicious fruit of love."

" By *l'abandon* I throw myself
Into Thine arms, my loving Lord."

months had passed since her act of oblation to the merciful love of God. Since that act of June 9th, 1895, her sole desire had been to live and to die in martyrdom to the love of God.

This martyrdom she conceived as a complete yielding up of herself to be consumed by God and to receive into her soul the pent-up streams of His infinite love.

Despite mistakes often made upon this point, it is clear that there is no necessary relation between this oblation, this martyrdom, this consumption, and suffering. The soul who thus offers herself to God does not have in view a life of suffering or trial. All that she does is to hand herself over without reserve to her Creator. Though the word holocaust might suggest it, her offering of herself as a victim does not mean her total destruction in pain or even annihilation, but the destruction in her of every obstacle to the free action of God's merciful love.

In other words, her offering of herself as a victim is a giving-over of herself to the perfect accomplishment of the Will of God. This act transcends the desire for suffering, as also any other particular desire, for all is now at the free disposition of God's infinite love. Yet it does not exclude the love of suffering when such is the Will of God.

It seems impossible to advance further. We speak often of the simplicity of the saint, but we must be careful to understand it aright. It does not mean an artificial simplification of spiritual problems through a failure to recognise their concrete reality, or through a determination to reduce them to elementary notions. It means rather the supreme touch of genius which finally always leads her, even though at first she is not quite sure of her approach, to the very heart of the problem and enables her to discover the principle that solves all difficulties.

Her complete yielding of herself to God is then her final solution of the problems of suffering and love. Other solutions, compared to hers, seem to be partial, theoretical or inadequate.

Those who, like Louis Chardon, assert a direct and necessary relation between progress in grace and longing for the Cross,[1] will cry out against the uprooting of the desire for suffering in the soul as it arrives at the final stage of its perfection. But we must admit that, however noble such a conception may be, it is one-sided and seeks to put constraint upon the free action of Almighty God.

Thérèse's attitude is more satisfactory. It recognises the incomparable value of the Cross, but it is careful not to substitute any means, even the most perfect, for what is the first and the last principle of all creation, the free Will of God. If God sends the Cross to Thérèse, she loves it and does not ask to be delivered from it. If He sends her joy, a life without pain, a foretaste of heaven, this, too, she loves as a gift from God and as powerful a means for saving souls as suffering, if she receives it with equal love.

From this point of view she seems at first sight to be in agreement with her master, St. John of the Cross. The doctor of *The Ascent of Mount Carmel, The Living Flame of Love,* and *The Spiritual Canticle,* speaks of the final stage of the soul's progress as a state that is beyond all power of description, for the reason that " here it is Our Lord Who communicates Himself to the soul and gives it an admirable glory that transforms it into Himself." [2] But here St. John goes beyond our saint. In the space at our disposal it would be too delicate and difficult a task to give a complete account of this state, but at least we can say that it seems to be conceived by the great doctor of mystical theology as something beyond the reach of trials. When the will " is identified by love with this devouring flame " (*i.e.,* the Holy Ghost), the soul, having now passed beyond the stages of the *Ascent of Mount Carmel* and the *Dark Night,* can address

---

[1] Cf. Louis Chardon, *La Croix de Jésus,* quoted by Père Garrigou-Lagrange, *L'Amour de Dieu et la Croix de Jésus,* I, 257: "the further these souls advance in their union with the spirit of Christ, the greater obligation do they contract to suffer." He goes on (p. 258) to speak of Our Lord as " being driven forward as by a heavy weight towards the Cross. *It is absolutely necessary, therefore, that this grace should create the same desire* and exercise the same force in souls who are predestined."

[2] *First Spiritual Canticle,* Str. XVII.

" this flame which now is so sweet to her," though " before it was for her a cruel suffering," and say:

> " O Divine Flame, not only are you no longer dark, as formerly, but you are the divine light of my understanding, the light by which I can contemplate you. Not only do you no longer make my weakness to faint, but you are, on the contrary, the strength of my will, by which I can love you and rejoice in you, being utterly transformed in you by divine love. Not only are you no longer the occasion of suffering and affliction for my soul, but you are its glory, its delight and its exaltation. Thus to me may now be applied the words of the Canticle: Who is she that comes up from the desert, filled with delights, leaning upon her Best-Beloved,[1] and diffusing love on all sides? " [2]

Such a union not only excludes aridities,[3] but includes happiness and glory.

> " Since the soul here rejoices in a life so happy and glorious, we may try to form an idea, if possible, of the incomparable delights with which it is inundated. As God Himself cannot suffer the slightest pain, so neither can the soul, in this condition, any more than He, suffer any. On the contrary, its most intimate substance is transformed in God and it is filled to overflowing with the delights and the glories of the Divinity, which bring to it an inexpressible happiness." [4]

We have but touched upon a comparison which deserves a far more detailed study, and yet we seem to be justified in saying that Thérèse's doctrine of complete self-abandonment to God has all the advantages and escapes the inconveniences of the two other positions which we have quoted as typical.

On the one hand, Louis Chardon's doctrine, by its definite and constant reference to the Cross, tends to exaggerate

---

[1] *Cant.* VIII, 5.
[2] *The Living Flame*, Str. I, v. 4.
[3] *Spiritual Canticle*, Str. XVII (explanation). Spiritual dryness is an enemy which now the soul forbids to enter, " barring the door against it, thanks to devotion and continual prayer."
[4] *Spiritual Canticle*, Str. XXII, (explanation).

the part of pain in the perfect life and thus to limit the
free action of God and minimize the participation of the soul
in Christ glorified.   On the other hand, through his idea
of the transformation of the soul in God—God Who can
suffer no grief nor be the subject of pain or affliction—
St. John of the Cross may seem to tend to free the perfect
soul from all kinds of darkness and even from all suffering,
and to suggest that any kind of trial, at least in the spiritual
order, is incompatible with the union of transformation.

Thérèse's teaching of complete self-giving to God, whilst
it takes no account of all the possible ways in which God
might act, seems to pass beyond St. John's scheme and yet
perfectly to realise it.   It seems to resolve this crucial
problem in a way that is more essentially theological than
the Doctor of spiritual marriage has done.   She does not
attempt to find in any psychological experience an anticipation
of the life of the blessed, but makes the highest action of
the soul to consist in the fullest self-surrender to the free
action of God's Will.   Thus she excludes any possibility of
illusion for she leaves herself unreservedly in the hands of
God.   Perhaps in this way she achieves for the first time,
more perfectly than in St. John's teaching, if not in his
life, perfect abnegation of spirit.

Nothing of self now remains in this elect soul.   She
had found rich treasures in suffering, but now she renounces
them and yields herself to love alone.   She knew that her
Spouse had been pleased to receive the rose petals of her
sufferings, because they expressed her love for Him, but now
she understood that her complete renunciation of self would
please Him still more.

Thus she reaches the final perfection of her spiritual life.
No longer is she attached by desire to any creature, even to
herself.   She is now absolutely at the disposal of the merciful
love of her Creator.

It is in this light that we must view the final trial of this
generous victim, if we would discover its full meaning.
If it is true to see in it Our Lord's reply to Thérèse's act

of self-oblation, it is still more true to see in it the final
question that divine Love can put here below to created
love—the dialogue most pathetic in its simplicity that the
inner history of souls has recorded since the Book of Job.
Thereby the young nun, who was to bring so many souls to
God, won her last victory over the insidious enemies of her
faith and her hope.

After six months of spiritual calm and stability, Thérèse,
at the beginning of April, 1896, experienced a sudden change.
As we know well enough, it was not then that suffering
first came to her, but then it was that she had to face the
three-fold martyrdom of body, heart and soul that Père
Petitot has so well analysed in some of the best pages of his
book.[1] I have already dealt with their relation to Thérèse's
conceptions of life and of love, and I need not repeat what
I have said.[2] Yet it will be well to point out the chief
characteristics of her last trial in the light of all that we have
now learned about this saintly soul and her destiny.

Thérèse's greatest trial came upon her at the beginning
of April, 1896, and lasted, without respite or break, until
her death. However superficially we regard it, we cannot
fail to be struck by the fact that it seems to be the contradiction
of all that was deepest and best in her. Without any attempt
at a complete analysis we can see at once five points on which
we might be tempted to think that God was trying to convince
her of rashness or even error, and to bring her back to a
right frame of mind by opposing her deepest desires and
convictions. We can go through them briefly.

Her faith in eternal life had always been so vivid and so
real that it was for her the central truth around which
everything revolved. Now a mocking voice kept saying to
her: " There is no heaven; you are destined to annihilation."

She had always regarded God as her most loving Father
and had given Him her fullest confidence. It was not long
since she had made her final discovery that He, the God of
love, was so infinitely merciful that His mercy as it were

---

[1] *op. cit.* Part II, C. 3.   [2] *Sup.* pp. 98.

absorbed His justice, and not long since she had made her act of complete self-oblation to that merciful love. But now, in that environment of infinite mercy and tenderness, she was suffering from the ravages of an incurable disease, and from the obtuseness of the Mother Prioress who, doubtless with the best intentions, often refused to allow her to have necessary attention and thus occasioned her the most acute suffering.[1] Moreover her interior trials were at their worst; she was threatened with the loss of her two sisters, Pauline and Céline who were to go to Saigon,[2] and all the while her young life was rapidly ebbing away.

To the God of love Thérèse had offered herself without reserve by an act of purest love. But if she had given herself up to Him, He in return seemed to have given her up. Despite one or two remarkable consolations, the almost unbroken rule was that she received no sign of protection, or of tenderness either for soul or body. The forces of dissolution and death, of temptation and darkness, were unchecked.

To give God the souls for whom He thirsted, Thérèse would have been ready to fly to the ends of the earth. The Mother Prioress considered that she had a true missionary vocation, though her illness made it impossible for her to carry it out.[3]

As the Carmel of Hanoï was repeatedly asking for her, she began a novena to Ven. Théophane Vénard in order that

---

[1] The evidence of Mère Agnès at the Apostolic Process is decisive on the point; cf. *Summarium*, paras. 2374-2375: "She had become so emaciated that in several places the bones had worked their way through her skin, and two most painful wounds had been formed. During the five weeks when Doctor de Cornières was on holiday, the Mother Prioress brought in Doctor La Néele only three times, although the latter said that she needed to see a doctor daily;" para. 2376: "From August 17th to 30th, she did not see a doctor, although there were serious complications"; para. 2377: "Doctor de Cornières returned in the early days of September, he spoke of injecting morphine, but the Mother Prioress would not allow it."

[2] Piat, *op. cit.* (p. 399).

[3] Letter cxci, to P. Roulland, March 19th, 1897: "Perhaps you would like to know what our Mother thinks of my desire to go to Tonkin? She believes in my vocation . . . but does not think it can ever be realized. For that the scabbard would have to be as strong as the sword."

she might be cured and obey the call.   This novena marked
the beginning of a grave relapse.[1]

On August 6th, 1896, the Feast of the Transfiguration,
a large picture of the Holy Face was placed over her bed:
it was surrounded by flowers and had a night light placed
before it.   Never did she suffer more from her temptation
against faith than on this night.[2]

Finally—and this brings us to the very heart of the
paradox—Thérèse knew perfectly well the classical teaching
of the Carmel upon the state of the soul which has arrived
at the highest degrees of union with God.   When she was
seventeen or eighteen years old she had read St. John of the
Cross and had derived much help from his works.[3]   But
according to that saint, the soul which has come to the
end of its spiritual progress and is nearing its heavenly home,
is so closely united to the Spouse Who is going to give
Himself so soon to her, that " God and the soul in this state
are but one," the soul being " entirely transformed in God." [4]
This transforming union must have its special consequences.
The following is but one of the many passages that might
be quoted:

> " The Spouse sings of the purity which the soul enjoys
> in this sublime state, of the riches which it has discovered
> and the glorious reward it has received, for having laboured
> so generously, for having spared neither toil nor sacrifices
> in order to reach it.   He celebrates the unspeakable
> happiness brought to it by its meeting with its Spouse in
> this divine union.   He describes the fulfilment of its desires,
> the sweet refreshment it enjoys, its inexpressible delights,
> now that it has escaped from the difficulties and the
> sufferings of its former life." [5]

---

[1] *A.* p. 220.   [2] Petitot, *op. cit.* p. 276.

[3] *A.* p. 147.   [4] *Spiritual Canticle*, Str. XXVI, (explanation).

[5] *Ibid*. Str. XXXIV (explanation).   It is clear from *N. V.* (pp. 134-140 and 128)
that a comparison with the saint was suggested to her: " Some one quoted, and
applied to her, the words of St. John of the Cross: ' Souls which have reached
perfect love can see without danger their own supernatural beauty.'   She replied:
' What beauty?   I can see in myself no beauty: I see but the graces I have received
from God ' " (cf. *The Living Flame*, Str. I).   The " sigh " mentioned on p. 139 teaches
the same lesson.

Unspeakable happiness, sweet refreshment, inexpressible delights— what a mockery for a soul tortured with triple martyrdom! Thérèse is indeed coming to the end of her pilgrimage. She knows it perfectly well. And yet at the end she is suffering this distress, this dereliction, this threefold martyrdom—all of which are the very opposite to the ecstatic descriptions of the most authoritative doctor of Carmel! How can she fail to see that in trying to be a great saint, and to win heaven by yielding herself up as a little child to the merciful love of God, she has been the victim of complete delusion.

Such was the sense, such the bearing, of this supreme trial. On its outcome depended the inauguration of a new era in the history of souls and of the spiritual life. We need not be surprised that the evil spirit employed all the resources of his most subtle strategy. The fate of an immense army of " little souls " was at stake whilst this faithful soul was engaged in her secret struggle. How grateful they should be to her for her victory on their behalf! They should look upon these weeks and months of her agony with profound awe.

For Thérèse has not only composed the charter of their liberation. By the certainty and security of her teaching, by her amazing victory over most fearful temptation, she has broken their chains and opened to them the way to the highest sanctity.

Thérèse, then, was suffering her triple martyrdom, and at first sight it seemed to be out of harmony with her doctrine, for her offering of herself to divine mercy was not an offering to His justice, nor did her offering to His love include the desire for suffering. Yet it was in this same doctrine and in her generosity and love that she found the weapons of her victory. She learned to cling more closely than ever to the adorable wisdom of the Father and to realise that it was a thousand times more infallible than her own love.

Her victory over the triple attack was the final proof of her magnificent sanctity and brought her all the fruits of salvation. It is easy to speak of yielding oneself unresistingly to God when a light breeze fills the sails of pure love and brings the barque into the desired haven. But it is very different in a hurricane! It is different when everything is lacking; still more when everything rises up in violent opposition to every movement of the heart!

It was when the tempest was at its height, it was when everything seemed lost or, more truly, when, humanly speaking, everything *was* lost, that there appeared the beacon-light of her luminous teaching.

On August 3rd, 1897, eaten up with pain, the " little victim of merciful love " asked for a pencil and wrote to her dear Sœur Geneviève, the following note:

> " O my God! How good Thou art to the little victim of Thy merciful love. Now that Thou dost add bodily pain to the inner sufferings of my soul, I cannot say: The agonies of death have surrounded me,[1] but I cry out in my gratitude: I have gone down into the valley of the shadow of death, yet I fear no evil because Thou art with me, O Lord." [2]

Was, then, Our Lord with her in her dereliction? Yes! And here she gained her most decisive and her most fruitful victory, for was it not her office to proclaim to all that it was sufficient to cling heroically to the three theological virtues and to the teaching of the Gospels, whatever the darkness that might invade the soul?

Not for one moment did she entertain the idea that God had really abandoned her, and more perfectly than ever did she yield herself without reserve to His merciful love. She made no distinction between what came to her from creatures and what was to be attributed to God,[3] or between what was to be resisted or rejected and what was to be welcomed, between what might be a punishment of God's justice and what was the worth of His love. She overlooked all secondary causes and accepted everything as part of God's plan. Nothing could shake the certainty of her faith that

---

[1] *Ps.* xvii, 5.   [2] *Ps.* xxii, 4.

[3] Cf. *The Spirit of St. Thérèse:* " Nothing appeared to her to come directly from creatures, neither joys nor pains: it was always the good God who had permitted whatever happened to her," etc. (p. 52-53).

He was love itself, and in the uttermost sincerity of her heart she cried out: Lord, all that Thou dost fills me with joy! [1]

She says: "all that Thou dost," and not "all that Thou allowest to happen or permittest others to do." Distinctions such as these might be necessary for the weak, but for the victim of God's merciful love they would bring neither light nor satisfaction. Everything comes to her directly from God. It is He Who works in her. He it is Who by consuming His little victim brings her to perfection.

Such treatment is not what was promised by her blessed father, St. John of the Cross. What did that matter? She had found peace in giving herself to God in perfect faith and she did not trouble to chart out the progress of her interior life nor to question the complete liberty of God to act as He would. Wherever she was, whatever happened, however long her trial lasted, it was God Who was working out His designs, and whatever He did she lovingly accepted.[2] "If my life is nothing but suffering," she said, "if the heavens are so dark that I can see no ray of light, in that I find my joy." [3]

Even if her prayers seemed almost a mockery she took refuge in deliberate and determined thanksgiving:

> "She admitted that when she prayed heaven to come to her help, it was then that she felt least help of all. When we expressed our surprise, she replied: 'But I am not in the least discouraged. I turn to God and to all the saints, and I thank them all the same. It seems to me that they want to see to what lengths I shall carry my trust. No! It is not for nothing that I have taken to heart the words of Job: Even though God should kill me, yet would I trust in Him." [4]

---

[1] A. Ch. IX, p. 157 (written in June, 1897). N. V. p. 61 (July 12th). The same phrase was written by her in June, 1897, on the last page of the book of the Gospels which she bore always upon her breast. She has underlined all. A facsimile is printed below the portrait which forms the frontispiece in the large edition of the Histoire d'une âme.

[2] N. V. p. 16. "I have no preference for death rather than life. I leave the good God to choose for me. Whatever He does I accept with love."

[3] N. V., p. 17.

[4] Sœur Geneviève at the Apostolic Process, Summ. p. 841. The text is quoted from Job xiii, 15. Cf. N. V., p. 42: "The words: 'Even though God should kill me, yet would I trust in Him,' have delighted me ever since my childhood. But it was a long time before I could reach such a degree of confidence. Now I have reached it. God has taken me into His arms and placed me there."

And then, secure in her own faith, she makes the darkness that would obscure it, into a source of light for those who had no faith. With all the strength of her will she forced herself to make numberless acts of faith[1] and offered them, together with her trial, to obtain the light of faith for unbelievers.[2]

Thus, in giving herself up absolutely to God's good pleasure she found the secret of being " always happy and contented." [3]   The words she uttered one day, in the simplicity and strength of her faith, clearly show that she entertained none of those depressing or pessimistic thoughts, the possibility of which we suggested some pages back:

> " I do not find it easy to see what more I shall have after my death than I already possess. . .   It is true that I shall see the good God, but, as for being with Him, that I already am upon the earth." [4]

Once more, Thérèse overcomes the hardest trials that could possibly assail a human life entirely consecrated to God, and thereby reveals to us a creative genius ranking with the very highest.

When her religious life seemed to be falling in ruins around her, when all the trust she had put in God seemed to be in vain, she took refuge in a complete and unconditional yielding up of herself to the Will of her heavenly Father. In all her interior and exterior trials she saw the direct, the personal action of the merciful love of God and a reason for loving Him all the more ardently. Her burning love,

---

[1] A. p. 157: " Though I have no joy in my faith, I force myself to put it into practice. I have made more acts of faith during the last year than during all the rest of my life."

[2] A. p. 156: " But, Lord, Thy child has understood that Thou art the light divine. She asks Thy pardon for her brethren who have no faith; she is willing to eat the bread of sorrow as long as Thou mayest wish. . . May all those, who hitherto have been blind to the light of the faith, at length accept its radiance. . . Even if it were possible that Thou shouldst remain in ignorance of my sufferings, I should still wish to endure them, in the hope that, by my tears, I might hinder, or at least make reparation for, one single sin committed against the faith.

[3] N. V., pp. 38 and 28: " I leave myself in God's hands and I am happy."

[4] N. V., p. 2.

though it no longer asked for suffering, accepted it and transformed it into the purest joy.

Wounded and crushed just at the time when she might have looked forward to the fullest and happiest development of her spiritual life, Thérèse, with supernatural wisdom, realised that in this final trial which brought her near to her crucified Lord, there was implied a last and all-important question from the merciful love of God. To this ultimate and supreme question, without hesitation or wavering, without any withdrawal from the beginning until the end, her love made reply:

"Yes, my God; yes, my God; I indeed will it all![1] To will all that God wills is love's last word."

We should be giving a distorted or even false idea of Thérèse's attitude towards suffering if we left out her devotion to Our Lady. She loved her as a mother and knew that her sovereign dignity did not exempt her from interior trials such as vex souls who are most closely united to God. Our Lady helped her to bear her sufferings with calmness, joy and the surest confidence. We have only to read the *Novissima Verba* to see the place the Blessed Virgin had in the life and thought of Thérèse during these last months.

On the first day of her month of May, Our Lady filled Thérèse's heart with heavenly joy.[2] A little later she obtained for her some physical relief.[3] To her Thérèse addressed her boldest prayers.[4] Into her hands she puts the requests she makes to God.[5] In the midst of all her trials, Thérèse loves

---

[1] *N. V.*, p. 184.

[2] *N. V.*, p. 1.

[3] *N. V.*, p. 19: "I prayed to Our Lady that I might get over the drowsiness and heaviness of these last days . . . to-day she has heard my prayer."

[4] *N. V.*, p. 20: "I should like to have a beautiful death in order to give you pleasure. I have asked Our Lady for it." Also p. 91: "You may be sure I shall not die during the night. I have a wish not to die at night and I have asked Our Lady for that favour;" and p. 135: "Last night I asked Our Lady that I might stop coughing so that Sœur Geneviève could sleep," and the following words, so typical of her: "but I added: If you do not hear my prayer, I will love you all the more."

[5] *N. V.*, p. 28: "Very often I ask Our Lady to tell the good God that He need not stand on ceremony with me. It is she who does my commissions."

Our Lady so much that she never loses sight of her.[1]   When she foresees the grief of her sisters after her death, her thoughts turn to Our Lady on Calvary.[2]   Our Lady is her last refuge.[3]

But especially, Our Lady was her model, for Thérèse refused to believe that the mother of Jesus had no experience of physical pain and spiritual trials.   In opposition to the opinion of a priest who held that Our Lady was exempt from pain, she did not hesitate to say:

> " As I gazed upon Our Lady's statue this evening, I understood that that was not true: I realized that she suffered much on her travels, from cold, from heat, from weariness. . .   Many a time she had to go without food. . . Yes, she knows what it is to suffer." [4]

Also it is a capital point in Thérèse's teaching upon Our Lady that the Son of God did not exempt His mother from the dark night of the soul and from anguish of heart.   Did He not allow her to spend three days in searching for Him? And when she was overjoyed at finding him again, did He not remind her that as a primary duty He had to be about His Father's business?   From this incident of the Gospel, Thérèse drew both a most practical lesson for herself and for all who have to walk in the darkness of faith or in anguish of heart, and also a powerful source of comfort:

> " The mystery of the Temple full well I comprehend
>   The answer, tone and manner of my most loving King.
> Mother, thou art the model of souls, unto the end,
>   Who seek Him in the darkness of faith and suffering.
> The all-wise King of Heaven would have His mother know
>   The night of faith submissive and agony endure.

---

[1] N. V., p. 47: " The Blessed Virgin will never be hidden from me, for I love her too much."

[2] N. V., p. 85.

[3] N. V., p. 154: " If we pray to Our Lady and she does not hear our prayer, we should leave her to act as she will and should have no further anxiety in the matter."

[4] N. V., p. 141-144.   Also her long exposition of her teaching on Our Lady, pp. 149-154.

Hence it is good to suffer, to taste the cup of woe;
  Yea, here to love and suffer is happiness most pure.
All that I have receivèd, Jesus may take again;
  Tell Him to treat me always as He may think most right.
And if He hideth from me, patient I shall remain
  Until that day undying when faith is lost in sight."

Until that day undying when faith is lost in sight. Taught by Our Lady, Thérèse could imitate her example, apply it to other circumstances and patiently endure her trial until the day of eternity should break upon her. In this strophe we may admire the doctrinal basis, its accurate rendering of the truths by which Thérèse lived, and the sure confidence of the concluding lines. Thérèse has here succeeded in ascribing to the Mediatrix of all graces an office that will increase men's love for her. She has described her as the model and the guide of all " little souls " who are sincerely seeking for God, but are unable to emerge from the dark night of their trials. Since the Son of God could give His mother nothing better than sorrow and darkness, how can we hesitate to walk in the same path?

The argument is sound, and the example forcible. The thought contained in these lines is not merely an idle imagination. She recited them again on July 11th, when " she was enduring great suffering because of her temptation against faith and her physical prostration." [1] They would help many a soul of weak faith to endure suffering. They would teach them to accept humbly all that God permits to come to them, and to await with loving confidence the day when God will say: " Now! It is My turn." They would strengthen them in their daily trials and at last lead them to the glorious day of eternity when their faith will be transformed into the open vision of God.

Thus was Thérèse enlightened, guided, and sustained by the Blessed Virgin as she approached the end of her life. It was impossible to doubt that it was indeed Our Blessed Lady whose smile had cured her as a child. It was that same

[1] N. V., p. 55. Mère Agnès adds: " Then she began to recite this strophe of her hymn to the Blessed Virgin."

tender mother who had now strengthened her in her anguish
and pain to utter her sublime *fiat*—the last word of her love.

Was it the last word? No, for she had still to die, and
Thérèse, like all other Catholics, had learned from the
Gospel that there is no greater love than to give one's life
for one's friends. The words used to ring in her heart.[1]
As a child she had often dreamed of giving her life in
martyrdom for her beloved Lord, and her pilgrimage to
Rome had been a powerful stimulus to her desire. We
cannot say when first the thought came to her of the happiness
of giving Jesus this last proof of her love, but we are able to
fix exactly the day on which she prayed for the grace of
martyrdom and felt a certainty of being heard. It was
Monday, November 14th, 1887.[2]
On that day Thérèse visited, with Céline, the monuments
" outside the walls." This is how she describes her emotions
when, despite the barriers, she made her way into the
Coliseum and kissed the ground:

> " My heart was beating violently as I pressed my lips
> to the dust reddened with the blood of the early Christians.
> I begged for the grace that I too might be a martyr for
> Jesus, and I felt in the depths of my soul that my prayer
> was heard." [3]

We may admire the heroism of the prayer and her assurance
of its being answered. Thérèse never turned back. She
was sure she would be granted her request, and far from

[1] John xv. 13. The text is quoted three times in the saint's published writings,
viz. *A.* p. 162 and pp. 371 and 400 in the French *Histoire d'une âme.*
[2] *A.* p. 112: " We spent six days in seeing the chief wonders of Rome, and on the
seventh I saw the greatest wonder of all—Leo XIII "; *A.* p. 110: " Our first day,
perhaps the most delightful of all, was spent outside the walls. . . I cannot express
how thrilled I was at the Coliseum. Now at length I was gazing at the arena where
so many martyrs had shed their blood for Jesus! " As then it was on Sunday,
November 20th, that the pilgrims from Bayeux had their papal audience, it follows
that Thérèse's visit to the Coliseum was on Monday, November 14th.
[3] *A.* p. 111: It is quite likely that the desire and the prayer were of an earlier
date. For five years her sister Pauline had borne the name of Agnès, and Thérèse
must certainly have known the story of that heroic little martyr; cf. p. 112: " My
visit to the church of St. Agnes was also a great consolation. In her I met again a
friend of my childhood."

retracting it, she never ceased to renew it. The day of her profession she bore upon her heart a note in which were written out her special intentions. In the centre stood these words:

> "O Jesus! May I die a martyr for Thee. Grant me martyrdom either of soul or body. Or rather, grant me both!" [1]

These were no idle words. One of the few ideas for which Thérèse expressly acknowledges her indebtedness to theologians is that the religious life is a martyrdom[2]—a long witness of love. Therefore did she live that life in its full rigour, so that it might lose no part of that character that was so dear to her. She accepted and loved all her sufferings, for they constituted that daily martyrdom.

But this was far from enough for such love. It did not seem likely that she would be called upon literally to die a martyr's death, although persecution was in the air, therefore she must commit the matter to God. That is why, in her act of oblation, she says, in so many words: " That thus I may become, O my God, a martyr to Thy love." [3] God would surely take the matter in hand, for His little spouse in her cell was inflamed with the desire:

> "Ah! Above all, I long to be a martyr. Martyrdom! It was the dream of my childhood and it has grown up with me in my little cell of Carmel." [4]

Her desire was to be realised, but in her own characteristic way; that is to say, not in any way striking to the imagination, or sensational, but purely interiorly. The only extraordinary greatness about it would be the greatness of heroic love.

Thérèse was not destined to stand up before the persecutors of the faith and to shed her blood for Christ, and yet she

---

[1] A. p. 136.
[2] A. p. 159: " The religious life, which theologians call a martyrdom."
[3] A. p. 448.　　　[4] A. p. 202.

was to be, in her " little way," a model that all could follow. It was for that reason that the Holy Ghost taught her gradually to bring together and finally to identify the two notions of love and death.   She must have rejoiced in such a lesson of freedom.

Can we assign to it a precise date? I should not like to say; but at any rate it was before the beginning of 1895. It is clearly expressed in a poem of fifteen stanzas in which Thérèse expounds her life's programme.   This poem is dated February 26th.   It is of exceptional merit.   *To live by love* is to share so closely in the life of Jesus Himself,[1] that even the holiest religious life could bring us no nearer to Him.   To live by love necessarily includes death—a death of love that is a veritable martyrdom, such a martyrdom as that for which she longs:

> " To love Thee, Jesus, is a fruitful loss,
>   My perfumes are all Thine, my love to prove,
> Oh, may I sing, when time's short stream I cross,
>   *I die of love.*
> To die of love, 'tis martyrdom divine,
>   For which my spirit thirsteth day and night;
> O Cherubim, attune your harps with mine,
>   Full soon from exile shall my soul take flight.
> O burning dart, consume me with thy fire,
>   Wound thou my heart, as lonely here I sigh,
> O Jesus, grant my dream, my one desire,
>   *Of love to die.*
> To die of love, ah! 'tis my hope most dear," etc.

From this moment, Thérèse had no need to wait for the axe of the executioner.   She is determined to offer to her Beloved, not now a mere passing sacrifice, but the supreme oblation of all that she is and has—of life itself, the last petal, so to say, of the rose.   Moreover, she knows that this sacrifice will have the value of martyrdom.

---

[1] From the poem *Vivre d'amour*.   Note the words:
    To live by love—ah! 'tis Thy life to live,
    O glorious King, in whom the elect rejoice, etc.

Why? Just because it will be a death *of love*. Whereas others fear death as the prince of terrors and recoil from it in horror, she will accept it as the Will of her heavenly Father, she will even love it as the gift of His merciful love, not directly because it leads to the glory of eternal life, but because it is in accord with the designs of His wisdom. Thus by her death she will bear her witness to God's truth, she will restore, so far as is in her power, the disorder brought about by Adam's disobedience, and she will be a martyr of love.

These lofty aspirations made her desire death as a true martyrdom. To the end she regarded it in this light, even when her desire gave place to a simple self-abandonment to the Will of God, for such an attitude includes the love of the martyr's death. It excludes only the desire to know when it is to come and to hasten its coming.

Sometimes, indeed, with that spice of humour that not infrequently enlivens some of her last words and writings, Thérèse tells people that she will *die of death*.[1] But this reference to the sentence passed upon our first parents is significant, for it hints at Thérèse's special conception of death. Just because she wanted to make of her death an act of love, she freed herself, as far as it depended upon her, from the effects of original sin, she approached as nearly as is given to a sinful creature, to the Immaculate Mother of God, and she grasped the true meaning of Calvary.

Now we can appreciate her generous words of hope:

> " In her poems she had sung of this death of love. In order to obtain it she had lived by love and was still living by it, her love proving itself as ever by her complete self-surrender in the midst of her sufferings. She wrote: ' I am quite content to be ill all my life if that gives pleasure to God, and I am even willing that my life should be very long. The only grace I ask is that I may die of love.' "[2]

---

[1] *N. V.*, p. 116: " Of what will you die?—But, I shall die of death. God did not tell Adam of what he would die; He said: Thou shalt die the death (*Gen.* ii. 17). That is quite simple."

[2] Deposition of Sœur Geneviève, *Summ.* p. 841.

> " She always had the hope, or rather the certainty that
> she would die of love: ' I am always hoping to die of love,'
> she said to us." [1]

Such a hope, one of the most beautiful in the spiritual
history of mankind, we may humbly hope to share. We find
it expressed again, by her dying lips, with utter certainty:

> " Even my smallest desires have been fulfilled . . . then
> the greatest of all, that I may die of love, is sure also to be
> realized." [2]

Yet we must put the question: what exactly is meant by
dying of love? Did Thérèse dream of experiencing, in her
last moments, delightful happiness, transports of joy,
ecstasies, raptures? From two points of view the question
is important. First, in regard to her own example and
teaching; second, for the historian of mystical theology,
in regard to the teaching of her father, St. John of the Cross.

It may be better to begin with this second point, on which
we have already touched. If we carry our study a little
further we shall be able to define better the position of
our saint.

Thérèse herself makes it necessary for us to treat of the
matter. A month before her death she spoke to Mère Agnès
of the powerful influence exerted on her mind and on the
whole of her religious life by two remarkable passages of
St. John:

> " ' Rend the veil of this glad meeting.' I have always
> applied these words to a death from love, such as I hope
> may be mine. Love will not wear out the veil of my life;
> it will suddenly rend it.
> " From the beginning of my religious life, I have repeated
> with keen desire and deep consolation these words of
> St. John of the Cross: ' It is of the very greatest importance
> that the soul should make numberless acts of love, so that

---

[1] Deposition of Mère Agnès, *Summ.* p. 865.
[2] *N. V*, p. 189-190.

it may be quickly consumed and not detained long here below, but come without delay to see its Creator face to face.' " [1]

It is undeniable, then, that St. John taught four important lessons to the little Carmelite of Lisieux. First, that the secret of growth in perfection is the constant exercise of love; second, that such an exercise normally leads to the speedy attainment of the beatific vision; third, that by its own power love prematurely breaks the bonds of such a perfect life; and fourth, that this breaking of the bonds is of the nature of a sudden disruption and not of a gradual erosion.

Thus her dependence upon the saint is certain. Yet as soon as we begin to define it we shall find that it is of limited degree, and that Thérèse's teaching has an originality of its own. Thereby, in spite of what seems a contradiction of St. John's teaching, she was enabled to stand firm and to be victorious in the gravest crisis of her spiritual life.

According to St. John of the Cross, love dissolved the union between the soul and the body. But a mystical theologian cannot be satisfied with stating the fact, he must put it in its due perspective and analyse it. This St. John does, and he assigns the dissolution to the final phase of spiritual marriage. Hence its essential characteristics; it is sweet, glorious, triumphant.

"The third veil now alone remains to be torn asunder, the veil of sensitive life. That is why one veil alone is here spoken of, and not several. There is indeed only one, and this flame encounters it, not in a grievous and painful manner as it encountered the two other veils, but with a gentleness that brings great delight to the soul. The death of these souls is accompanied with marvellous sweetness and consolation which far surpass all they have experienced during the whole course of their spiritual life. They die, wounded by love's darts, in delicious ecstasy, as the swan sings most melodiously when it is at the point of death.

---

[1] N. V., p. 88, quoting The Living Flame, Str. I.

> That is why David wrote that the death of the just is precious in the eyes of God.[1] Then it is that the streams of love burst their bounds in the soul and hasten to lose themselves in the ocean of divine love. They are there so mighty and powerful that they already seem like the sea. The soul sees . . . that it is as pure and as rich as faith and the conditions of this life permit. . . For in this condition, God allows souls to see their own beauty." [2]

Where do we stand? If this is the death by love which Thérèse learned from St. John of the Cross; if this is the kind of death she desired as her martyrdom of love, then it is clear that she did not attain to it and that her greatest hope was frustrated.

But, on this vitally important point, there can be no possible room for doubt. It is absolutely certain that this was not the kind of death to which Thérèse looked forward as a death from love. She did not expect to see any part of St. John's description granted to her in answer to her prayers. Her teaching was just as consistent as his, and from it she was able to evolve, first for herself and then for those who should follow in her " little way," a conception of a death by love utterly deprived of any consolation which might lessen the merit of its heroic faith or be a present reward to its generous self-sacrifice. Others, even around her, may have been deceived. She, however, who had learned so well the lesson of utter detachment was not going to act inconsistently with that principle now that she had arrived at the final stage of her journey.

The love of which she speaks and sings, by which she lived and wished to die, had nothing to do with her feelings or her emotions. It was a pure act of the will, an act of utter detachment, an act of acceptance, in blind faith, of whatever was ordained by God's holy Will. Her will did not seek for

---

[1] *Ps.* cxv. 5.

[2] *The Living Flame,* Str. I, v. 6. " Rend the veil of this sweet encounter " is explained in the translation of the Carmelites of Paris thus: " These veils, which must be torn asunder in order perfectly to possess God, can be reduced to three. . . The third, which is sensitive, merely represents the union of the soul with the body."

direction in any system, but only in the gradual unfolding of God's designs. It sought for no light save the obscure light of faith.

Acting thus, Thérèse was sure of her way, sure of being in the path of love, even though no consolation or bright vision enlightened her. She dearly loved Our Lord indeed, but with such peace and self-forgetfulness that it would be more correct to say that she rested in His good pleasure rather than that she eagerly yearned to possess Him:

> " You do not know how calm the thought of going soon to heaven leaves me. Naturally, I am very happy, but I cannot say that I experience vivid joy or ecstasies of anticipation.
>
> " ' Yet you would prefer to die rather than to live? '
>
> " O mother dear, I repeat: no, I do not prefer one thing to the other. Whatever the good God prefers to choose for me, that is what most pleases me." [1]

The last word, then, of her love is to love death, if God sends it, and to prefer life if God wishes to prolong it. But as all the indications point to death as God's choice, it is for death that Thérèse prepares. That being so, is she in harmony with St. John of the Cross at least in her anticipations of her last moments of life?

Not in any way; and this difference, of which she is fully conscious, is a tacit appeal to the Gospel as the ultimate standard of Christian faith and hope.

Leaving to St. John the responsibility and the credit for his flamboyant descriptions, Thérèse looks far higher for the model which every Christian must follow, and for the teaching which is absolutely sure and without danger of illusion. Her model is Christ upon the Cross. She draws her lesson from the extreme reticence or even the silence of the Gospels as to the interior dispositions of our crucified Lord. Thérèse could not doubt that He Who was love itself had died of love and therefore she contemplated His death. She knew that His death was the source of all graces, and

---

[1] N. V., p. 167.

therefore from His death she begged the grace to be conformed to Him in the manner of her own death.   But:

> "Our Lord died upon the cross in bitter anguish, and yet His death was the most beautiful death through love that the world has ever seen. To die of love is not to die in ecstasy. . . I tell you frankly; it seems to me that that is what I am experiencing." [1]

She is quite clear about it. If death from love is to be Christ-like, it will exclude any extraordinary or consoling manifestations, it will probably involve very great suffering. Her words in this connection are most characteristic:

> "Do not be surprised if I do not appear to you after my death and if you do not receive any extraordinary sign of my happiness. You must remember that it is in the spirit of my ' little way ' to wish to have no visions . . . do not be distressed if I have much pain to suffer and if you do not see in me, as I have already told you, any sign of happiness at the moment of my death . . . Our Lord died as a victim of love, but see how fearful was His agony! " [2]

.   .   .   .   .

But it would be a serious misunderstanding of the nature of Thérèse's turning to the Gospel, to interpret it as a contradiction or disparagement of the teachings of mystical theology. On the contrary, by insisting on what was essential in them, she showed how valuable they were and how they could be extended and adapted to all men of good will.

In the system of St. John of the Cross, indeed, it seems inexact to speak, in the full sense of the words, of a death by love. It is true, of course, that the ardour of charity breaks the thread of human life, and that it is by the power of the Holy Ghost that man's love acquires that ardour. But it is none the less true that the separation of soul and body is considered merely as a passage from this world to the next and not as having any value in itself. We should

---

[1] N. V., p. 37.   [2] N. V., p. 19 (her farewell to her three sisters).

note, too, that according to his teaching, spiritual marriage, in so far as it is an anticipation of eternal happiness, of the mysteries and of the very life of the Most Holy Trinity, empties death of all importance and of all mystical meaning.

But with St. Thérèse of the Infant Jesus it is quite otherwise. With her it is death itself, this universal experience, that is invested with the very highest mystic value. Quite apart from any extraordinary phenomena, death in itself, the separation of body and soul, can be made a most perfect offering of love, because, in a way, it is truly the direct work of God's love. It is because death comes to her as a gift from God's love that she can die of love. Her faith has taught her that death must be regarded as a punishment by God's justice, yet she sees in it a design of God's infinite mercy, and, more profoundly still, the last question that His love puts to hers.

Though death destroys not only all her dreams, including that of shedding her blood for Christ, but her life itself, she lovingly embraces it as a gift from God's merciful love. God wishes it for her; her wish is as His. In wishing it as God wishes it, in this death by love she finds God Himself.

Not a God Who anticipates the normal course of events and reveals Himself to her before calling her from life and thereby softens the horror of death, although she cannot be exempted altogether from it, but a God Who, though still hidden from her, shows her the true meaning of her agonizing death.

" Thérèse, do you love Me? Do you love Me more than yourself? Do you love Me more than those loved Me, who needed, even in life, to be consoled by a foretaste of eternal joys? Do you love Me so dearly in those whom I have made My brethren, that for their salvation and to fill up the things that are wanting in My Passion, you love suffering and even death itself? Thérèse, do you love Me in the darkness of your faith, amidst the violent assaults upon your hope, in the slow and agonizing dissolution of your body? Thérèse, it is My love that is consuming your body: in dying, Thérèse, do you love Me? "

To her crucified Lord, Whose image she clasped in her hands, with her last breath she murmured: " My God, I love Thee." To all Our Lord's questions she answered " Yes." Thus did she die of love and made of her death a veritable martyrdom.

In her unfailing love of the Cross, in the fulness of her gratitude and in her eager desire to share in the work of redemption, she accepted death, with all that it implied, because it was the most perfect gift she could make to the God of love. Thus did she render to her hidden Lord the most sublime testimony that it was in the power of Christian faith and love to offer.

By her humble death of love she has taught us to see in the decrees of eternal justice the workings of infinite mercy. In suffering and even in death, she found not only the fruitfulness and the joy of her life, but also the opportunity to bear witness to God. For all men, who must face suffering and death, she has become the teacher, because she was the martyr, of His merciful love.

By their attitude to suffering and death we form our judgment of men, of doctrines, and of civilization itself. By her attitude to suffering and death, Thérèse is shown to us as God's own answer to the agonizing doubts of humanity. Whereas so many men rise up in rebellion, wander from the path of truth and are lost, Thérèse opened her soul to grace, accepted God's revealed truth with the fullest faith and made it the rule of her life. What she learned from the Gospels and from Our Lord in the Holy Eucharist is so perfect that we are constrained to admire it as the most beautiful flower of theology. We have but to portray it, in its simple truth, to realise that God wished to make of this child, at once so simple and yet of a genius so astounding, the martyr and the doctor of His merciful love.

Such a witness was never so needed as at the present time. We must never be wearied of studying and spreading abroad her testimony.

As we draw now to our conclusion, after having said so

much, and yet, in one sense, all too little, we would like to point out that we have tried to study the inspiration and the characteristics of the *martyr*, rather than give a complete and systematic *exposé* of the teaching of the *doctor*. For that reason we might be blamed for a certain distortion of Thérèse's message, or for allowing some of our readers to be discouraged at the sight of an exceptional sanctity so far beyond them, rather than encouraged by her example to follow her " little way." If, however, our readers will bear in mind the precise object at which we have aimed, we hope that they will spare their criticisms.

Yet we may help to obviate any misunderstandings and to put before our readers the authentic spirit of Thérèse's teaching, if in conclusion we call attention to a remarkable coincidence between her own personal experience and all that is most valuable, helpful and consoling in her teaching.

The life and the teaching of the saint form so harmonious a whole that it is impossible to exaggerate, still less to isolate, any one element in them without fatal results. I have dwelt at length on Thérèse's greatness, and therefore 1 have rejected the phrase which has gained currency, " the asceticism of littleness." But what 1 said on that point would be as dangerous as the view 1 was combating, more dangerous perhaps, if it were not balanced by a further consideration. I will treat of it here, out of its chronological order, so that I may give it its due emphasis.

It is characteristic of Thérèse's teaching that she destroys all illusions of human pride, and attributes the highest value to the humble dispositions of a sincere heart, provided that they are inspired and sustained by the example of Jesus, and by loving confidence.

We have followed the main lines of Thérèse's progress, the gradual change for her of suffering into joy, then into a complete gift of herself to God, and finally into a holocaust of pure love, this leading up to and including her death. But does her teaching imply that all of us, in the same degree, must pass through the same stages?

It would be most dangerous to think so. She was chosen from all mankind to point out the path to numberless followers of her " little way," but her own personal graces were very different from the teaching that she is qualified to give to each single member of this vast multitude. And for each one—save for those who trust in their own spiritual resources[1]—she gives guidance in accordance with their special vocation and graces.

When she was on earth, she could distinguish with the sureness of genius, the various stages of the spiritual life to which souls attained, together with the graces that accompanied them. Now that she is in heaven she acts in a similar way with all those troubled and tempted souls who ask her aid and so often shrink from the Cross.

When her father was so grievously stricken, she wrote to her sister Céline:

> " The thoughts of Jesus are not as our thoughts, nor His ways as our ways. He offers to our lips a chalice as bitter as our weak human nature can support . . . let us not refuse to taste this chalice prepared for us by the hand of Jesus. We must see life in its true light. It is an instant between two eternities. We must suffer in peace. I own that this word ' peace ' used to seem to me too strong, but the other day as I was meditating upon it, I found the secret of suffering in peace. Peace is not the same as joy, at any rate joy that can be felt. To suffer in peace, all that is needed is to will all that Our Lord wills." [2]

" All that is needed? " We should say rather " all that would be needed " if our heart were not suffering any other anguish. If it resigns itself not to feel joy, how can it resist the onslaught of sadness and disgust? Still more, can it be content to test its weakness unless love spurs it on to

---

[1] And God knows how she always distinguished in herself, with a great dread of illusion, the limits of her own strength, which in her humility she judged to be very little, and the abundant support of God's grace.

[2] Letter lxiii, April 4th, 1889, partly quoted in *A.* p. 336.

generosity? And if it fails under the trial, how can it escape being sunk in despair?

It is here that Thérèse's solution of the problem is so practical, so inexhaustible and so fruitful. It begins by unmasking the hidden self-love which seeks for these human satisfactions, and then it sows in our heart the Gospel seed which soon will bring forth the fruit of complete self-abandonment into God's hands.

She adds the idea of sorrow to that of suffering and arrives at the complex notion of complete suffering. Yet as Our Lord endured this complete suffering for our redemption, she bids those who suffer to think, not of their own miseries, but of Our Lord, and to unite themselves with Him. Even though He wills to leave us upon this earth, He never fails to support our weakness and to requite our love:

> "Let us not imagine we can love without suffering, and bitter suffering, too. We have our human nature and it cannot be ignored. But what great treasures suffering helps us to gain. It is our fortune, our livelihood; it is so precious that Jesus came upon the earth for the express purpose of possessing it. We must suffer even without consolation or courage. . . 'Jesus suffered sorrowfully. Could, indeed, the soul suffer unless it were in sorrow?' We should like to suffer generously and nobly; we should like never to fall. What an illusion! What does it matter, O my Jesus, if I fall every moment? Thereby I see my weakness and that is a great gain, while Thou seest what I can do and then Thou art more ready to bear me in Thine arms. If Thou dost not do so, it is because it pleases Thee to see me remain fallen upon the ground. In that case I shall not be distressed, but shall stretch out my arms lovingly and imploringly towards Thee. I will never believe that Thou wilt abandon me. . . 'It was when the saints were at the feet of Our Lord that they met their cross ' . . . Céline dear, sweet echo of my soul, if only you knew my misery." [1]

[1] Letter lxv, to Céline, April 1889, partly quoted under a different date in A. p. 336. The quotations are words of Pére Pichon, S.J., director of Thérèse's elder sisters. She also had confessed to him.

When later on, by her suffering and her *agonizing,* Thérèse had passed beyond this earlier stage and reached the point where she could give herself to God with complete self-abandonment, she would still recall its necessity and its laws to souls who still needed it:

> " Remember the words of the priest: ' The martyrs suffered with joy and the King of martyrs suffered with sorrow.' Yes, Jesus said: My Father, let this chalice pass from me.[1]

> " It is a great consolation to us to think that Jesus, the strong Son of God, experienced all our weaknesses, that He trembled at the sight of the bitter chalice, that chalice which in earlier days He had so ardently desired to drink." [2]

To-day, her mission is to teach all men these fundamental truths. In her school there is no room for arrogant presumption, nor for natural virtues, however specious, without charity, still less for discouragement or despair. Even if we should remain, temporarily or permanently, incapable of regarding intense suffering as our highest happiness, we may console ourselves with the thought that Christ, the Son of God, Himself trembled.

But when those who follow Thérèse in her " little way " are tortured by suffering, have they no other remedy than to recall Our Lord's bitter Passion and " to stretch out their arms lovingly and imploringly towards Him "?

No, for the final word of Thérèse's teaching is not to resign oneself " to remain fallen upon the ground," but to be certain that suffering is, in itself, the prelude to the glory of eternal life:

> " The day will come when shadows will disappear; then nothing will remain save joy and delight." [3]

---

[1] Letter clxxvi, to Sœur Marie, September 17th, 1896. The priest is Père Pichon. Cf. *A.* p. 360.

[2] Letter clxxxiv, to Abbé Bellière, December 26th, 1896. Cf. *A.* p. 369 (date corrected).

[3] Letter lxv, to Céline, April 26th, 1889 (fragment omitted in *A.* p. 340).

Thérèse's example here reinforces her words.   Her love for " little souls " will not allow her to consider herself as an exception.   Whoever will share in her humiliation will share also in her glory.   She wishes to make known to all the loving secrets of her Spouse.   The greatest of these has been revealed to the " poor little unfledged bird " by " the divine Eagle."   If only " the poor little creature," in the full knowledge of its weakness, will abandon itself to " the Eagle " who alone can bear it up, then—wonder of wonders—the victim consumed by love will be clothed with glory in the bosom of the adorable Trinity.[1]

Such was the destiny of Thérèse, and such, in due proportion, she assures us, will be the destiny of all who will yield themselves unreservedly and with complete confidence to the infinite mercy of God.

Such is the reward of suffering accepted with humility, borne with utter self-abandonment to God, and transfigured by love.

---

[1] For the whole of this conclusion, cf. *A.* p. 207-208.

POSTSCRIPT

PÈRE Gabriel de Ste. Marie-Madeleine, O.C.D., in September, 1947, published in the *Rivista di vita spirituale*, an article under the title of "Vita e morte di amore," the second part of which, "La morte di amore," agrees in essentials with my interpretation of St. Thérèse's death. He has now read the proofs of this chapter and kindly offered me his valuable observations. They have suggested some minor alterations in my work and also the following explanations:

1. The parallel that I have sketched between St. John and St. Thérèse has regard, not precisely to St. John's teaching as he himself lived and taught it, or as it can be found in the critical editions and translations, but to his teaching as Thérèse found it in the only translation at her disposal. I have confined myself to quoting from that translation in the actual copy of the Carmel of Lisieux. It consists of two volumes bound in one. It is a *New Translation made from the Seville edition of 1702*, and published by the Carmelites of Paris in 1875. The first volume contains Letters of P. Berthier and the *Spiritual Canticle* (Str. I-XXIX), and the second the *Spiritual Canticle* (Str. XXX-XL), the *Living Flame* and two sermons preached by Mgr. Landriot, Archbishop of Rheims, to his Carmelites in 1867 and 1872.

2. My problem, then, was not to define St. John's teaching in itself, but to show how St. Thérèse came to understand and to take up her remarkable position, although the texts of St. John, upon which she was nourished, did not seem to help her to reach it (although other members of the community based their hopes on these texts). My discussion, far too short, was not meant to be, nor thought to be, a complete analysis of the delicate question which I thought it opportune to suggest.

3. Every comparison which is only partial may be an occasion of error, and therefore I wish to emphasise the

qualifications I have already made in my text. Whatever may be the modifications demanded, it seems already abundantly clear that the mystical teachings of St. John and St. Thérèse respectively are not identical as regards the final phase of the spiritual life in this world, unless one violently brings them into agreement by a *tour de force* that seems without any justification. Whether we should simply accept the fact of their difference without comment, or whether we should consider Thérèse as having gone beyond, or fallen short, of St. John, is a further, and important, question which cannot be decided until the fundamental study to which I refer has yielded its results. It will be fairly clear which solution 1 am inclined to adopt. Even a cursory glance at the texts bearing on the matter which Thérèse had under her eyes (for example, *Spiritual Canticle,* Str. XXXIX, *Living Flame,* Str. I, vv. 1 and 5, II, vv. 4 and 6, III, v.1, etc.) will be sufficient to show how difficult it seems to me to be not to admit Thérèse's fundamental originality in a matter where the slightest vagueness of thought or the slightest hesitation of her will might have gravely compromised the balance of her life and the purity of her message.

4. In the preface which Père Gabriel is doing me the honour of contributing to the Italian translation of this present work (Editor: Commendatore Mario Calvelli, Florence), he will, with his customary skill, blaze out the trail which I have not yet had to follow.

KEY TO REFERENCES

A. *Autobiography of St. Thérèse of Lisieux (Histoire d'une âme).*

N.V. *Novissima Verba.*

LAVEILLE, CANON, *Sainte Thérèse de l'Enfant-Jésus.*

MOREAU, CANON PH., *Sainte Thérèse de l'Enfant-Jésus, Son temperament moral.*

PETITOT, HENRI, O.P., *Vie intégrale de Sainte Thérèse de Lisieux.*

PIAT, STEPHANE-JOSEPH, O.F.M., *Histoire d'une famille.*
(Translation: *The Story of a Family: The Home of St. Thérèse of Lisieux.* New York, Kenedy, 1947).

TRAVERT, CANON PAUL, *La souffrance, son origine et son rôle d'après Sainte Thérèse de l'Enfant-Jésus.*